West
Surrey
Architecture
1840 – 2000

Christopher Budgen

In association with
The Godalming Trust,
The Haslemere Society,
The Farnham Society

Heritage of Waverley Ltd
2002

First published in the
United Kingdom in 2002
by Heritage of Waverley Ltd
The Hollies Woodham Road Woking
Surrey GU21 4EN

*Type setting
and cover design by
Philip Hodkin*

Printed by Ian Allan Printing Ltd.
Riverdene Business Park, Molesey Road, Hersham,
Surrey KT12 4RG

ISBN 0 9542131 0 6

2002

Contents

Illustrations

Acknowledgements

My thanks to all who helped to make this book possible, especially the owners of the buildings featured. In particular I would like to thank Sir Robert and Lady Clarke, Tony and Shula Laws, Russell and Claire Clapshaw, Anita Morris and Jean-Paul Marix Evans. My thanks also to those researchers who assisted in the identification of buildings in their area, in particular Ben Pite, Janet Balchin, Audrey Monk, Michael Harding and Hugh Turrall-Clarke. Thanks are also due to those who kindly helped with financial assistance, either through grants, loans or subscriptions. In particular I would like to thank Waverley Borough Council, the R.I.B.A, Surrey Historic Buildings Trust and Hugh Turrall-Clarke. Thanks also to Michael Olliffe at Modern Design Group, Eileen Skwara at Surrey History Centre, Frances Barnes at Surrey County Council's Construction Management and Henry Chetwynd-Stapylton. My thanks also to the staff at Harvey Ide's for their help with photographic reproduction and unfailing good humour. Thanks too to Jonathan Bingham and the staff at Ian Allan and to Phil Hodkin for his work on the text, illustrations and cover design. My thanks to Michael Wilson and John Greenwood for permission to use the photographs of Snowdenham Hall.

Finally I would like to offer my sincere thanks to the members of The Godalming Trust, The Haslemere Society and The Farnham Society who worked long and hard to make this book a reality. In particular I would like to thank those closest to the project for their fine work - Alan Brown, Robert Serman, Ronnie Broughton, Hubert de Lisle and Terry Hone.

Foreword

The idea of documenting and recording the extensive but surprisingly little known architectural heritage of South West Surrey was born in 1995 when I was working with Roderick Gradidge. We used to travel together to meet clients and he had a rather battered A-Z map of the area on which he had marked all the noteworthy houses and the names of the architects involved. There was not a single page without several marks, and the south-west part of the county, the area covered by the Borough of Waverley, was the most intensely logged.

As a Waverley Councillor since 1991, I have spoken many times in Council about this unique inheritance, and have quoted Roderick's belief that we in this part of Surrey have the great good fortune to possess the best and most numerous examples of late Victorian and Edwardian country houses anywhere in the world. I have long believed that this fact was so significant that people should be made aware of it.

When in 1995 I had the honour of being elected the Mayor of Waverley, I determined that I would do something to promote this. As a member of both the Farnham Society and the Godalming Trust I knew well what talent and expertise local amenity societies could offer, and I therefore turned to them for help.

In February 1996 I arranged a meeting in the Mayor's Parlour for representatives of the Farnham Society, the Godalming Trust, The Haslemere Society and Cranleigh Parish Council. The meeting was attended by Roderick Gradidge, our MP Mrs Virginia Bottomley, the President of the RIBA Owen Luder, the Director of the Surrey Institute of Art and Design Professor Norman Taylor, Waverley's Planning and Development Manager Stephen Thwaites and his team, and many others. Following this launch, the Farnham Society under the chairmanship of Mary Nevile initiated a series of meetings of the three amenity societies, and the idea of "Roderick's" map as it became known, began to take shape.

A great many hours of labour have now gone into the project, resulting in this marvellous record of Waverley's architects and their work. It is an essential companion and source of information for all, architects and non-architects alike. The book is a reflection of the widespread interest in architecture which has grown over the years.

It gives me the greatest satisfaction that the inaugural meeting six years ago has borne this fruit, and I take especial pleasure in the knowledge that Waverley's amenity societies have worked together to produce it.

Local amenity societies always have a vital role to play in the protection and enhancement of their area, and thanks to the commitment and dedication of so many people this book is a remarkable achievement. I am proud to have been one of those who helped to launch it.

Michael Blower
September 2001

Introduction

"I stood before her and the nervous strain made my blood run cold. I questioned the picture, accused it, caressed it, prayed to it, called it mother, sweetheart, whore and strumpet, I called it Abraxas"
Hermann Hesse.

Art seeks from its audience an emotional response, and preferably a positive one; but more, much more than that, it seeks to elicit a spiritual response. Historically, art has sought to take man out of the mundane world, to transport him, at least for a while, to a higher, more knowing state. When Hesse's Sinclair stood before the portrait that he had created and questioned its meaning, its reason for being; he moved from being merely its observer to something approaching a state of grace.

And Art can do this, whether it be a painting, music, or architecture; for architecture too is an art. And since art reflects man's social condition, there have been times – and the sixties and seventies spring to mind – when the dividing line between architecture and mere building has become extremely thin, when the crass and the merely awful threatened to overwhelm the entire edifice of architectural endeavour. But the thing about architecture, as opposed to painting or sculpture, is that buildings are built to serve purposes other than that of art, they are built to be lived in, worked in and prayed in, and must fulfil this function before all else but it is perhaps when this primary function becomes a means to an end that architecture ceases and building begins.

This review takes a necessarily broad sweep through the history of architecture in an attempt to give the reader a flavour of the ideas that gave rise to the differing styles of the last few centuries without becoming too bogged down in the minutiae of each and every variation of design. It begins arbitrarily enough at the beginning of Victoria's long reign, at a time when the equally long reign of neo-Classicism was beginning to ebb and Pugin's Gothic Revival about to take England by storm. Before the century was out, England was recognized as the centre of architectural endeavour, its architects lauded abroad, their work copied in Europe and America. From this high point, in common with art in general, architecture went through some difficult times as it sought to reflect the horrors of the early twentieth century, at length to emerge into more favourable climes at the end of the millennium, its honour intact but still answerable to its final master – money (or rather the lack of it). Those architectural practitioners produced some of their best work in West Surrey and it is this body of work that this volume has sought to bring to book.

It is this conflict with money, with finance, with the perennially tight budget of the patron that has always dogged art, and architecture in particular. As early as 1892, the increasingly professional approach to architecture triggered open conflict within the architectural community and led to the famous treatise edited by Shaw and Jackson entitled, *Architecture – A profession or an Art*. As far as the architectural world was concerned it was an insoluble question and the row has rumbled on ever since. As Richard Scott, great-grandson of Sir George Gilbert Scott remarked in an article in the 1970s, "Art is a terrible word – it frightens us. In architects it conjures up visions of immoral grandeur and for clients – the patrons of architecture – it is something unfamiliar, and anyway how much would it cost?"

The research which underpins this book was begun by three civic societies in West Surrey – The Farnham Society, The Haslemere Society and The Godalming Trust - in the mid-nineties and initially planned as a millennium project to make a record of the area's architecture but, as is the way with these things, it has grown somewhat to its present format. Other work has been carried out by local history groups and interested individuals. That some areas appear to be over or under represented reflects the amount of research carried out in those localities rather than the amount of architecture present in each area. What has become clear from the research is the extreme difficulty of identifying the architect of particular buildings. While past owners tend to show up in deeds and other legal documents, the original drawings for these buildings have almost always long been lost, if indeed they were ever held by the original owners in the first place.

The appendix which holds the bulk of the research covers the entire borough of Waverley (and some others adjacent) and is arranged by civil parish. Each entry includes the name of the building, its architect and approximate date of construction; approximate because it is difficult to place a date on the exact moment in time that a building comes into being: is it the date that it is designed? the date that building commences? or finishes? or when it is occupied? All that can be said of the dates therefore is that they identify a point somewhere between when a building was first designed and its subsequent completion.

A cursory look at the life span of the architects featured will reveal that a disproportionate number of them were born in the mid nineteenth century and died around the time of the Second World War. This should not surprise us for these architects were fortunate to be practising their art in what was the greatest flowering of architecture for several hundred years. In comparison to those who came later, they were blessed with budgets and clients that allowed rather more ambitious designs and for whom ostentation was not yet quite the dirty word that it later became. Conversely, twentieth century architects have always had to put money squarely at the top of their priority list which can make for some uninspired designs. Also, since the war, and even before, it has become common for the architect to work as part of a practice, a move that has tended to conceal his identity rather more than he would have wished.

One of the great joys of the research for this book has been the immense kindness shown me by the owners of the properties featured here and hearing their stories. I especially liked the tale of the devoted couple that rang from the other side of the world, very keen to view the house of one of the great masters. Eventually the day arrived for their long anticipated visit to the great man's house and all started well but then their initial looks of puzzlement slowly turned to horror as it dawned on them that they had travelled thousands of miles to view the wrong house – that they were looking, not at Webb's Red House but at the Red House of some upstart called Lutyens.

The feeling that I have received from the owners of these properties is not so much pride but a sense of duty, of stewardship in that ownership. They, more than anyone, understand the value of what they possess and the costs involved in keeping them in good order. That is not to say that previous owners have always been quite so understanding. One had attempted to make his roof watertight by applying prodigious quantities of roofing felt which, to ensure it did not move, was firmly nailed down – straight through the leadwork that he was trying to repair. The next storm brought such a deluge through the roof that the damage is still evident years later. But the thought was there!

It is inevitable that this book will contain omissions and errors, it is in the nature of the work, but it is hoped that it may provide a starting point for a more complete survey of the superb architectural history that West Surrey is fortunate enough to harbour and we are lucky enough to enjoy.

Lastly, I would ask all readers to respect the privacy of the owners of the buildings illustrated here. While they have been kind enough to open their buildings for the purposes of this book, they will certainly not appreciate the world beating a path to their collective doors.

Christopher Budgen 2001

A SHORT HISTORY

The history of architecture in England since the collapse of the Roman Empire had been one of essentially vernacular styles. At times, continental forms, poorly grasped or completely misunderstood, had influenced indigenous designs but architectural forms had been broadly and unashamedly home grown. But then, the world went mad.

In eighteenth century England a most extraordinary thing happened; one so odd that at first it was incomprehensible, for it represented "…nothing more or less than the imposition of the temple architecture of an extinct Mediterranean civilization upon the house design of a northern people." So far reaching and all embracing was this event that no-one was able to avoid it, even the parson, "…deputy of Christ, lived behind a façade which was conceived in the terms of a Classical Order, entered his home through a doorway deriving from the portico of a pagan shrine and sat at a hearth which resembled a miniature triumphal arch or an altar to the Lares…" What was this revolution and whatever had happened to cause such sociological upheaval?

Its name was Palladianism, after Andrea Palladio, an Italian architect of the sixteenth century whose designs were based upon Roman forms and whose work, *I Quattro Libri dell' Architettura*, was reprinted in England in 1715. An enthusiasm for Roman forms, partly sparked by the first excavations at Roman Pompeii, was taken up by influential patrons such as Lord Burlington who commissioned houses in the Palladian style based on the *Villa Almerico* at Vicenza to produce houses totally unlike traditional English forms. Palladianism quickly ousted the relaxed indigenous styles and substituted one based on form and order. Palladianism was the architectural equivalent of the Age of Reason; it was intellect transfigured into mathematical proportion and precision. It was a shockingly modern style, completely at odds with the homeliness of Baroque or Gothic. This was an embodiment of orderliness, of regulation, of reason and it was applied to almost every new building, and not a few old ones, for the next 150 years.

Central to Palladianism, and the Georgian style that grew out of it, was a search for composition and proportion in architecture, a search that mirrored the Age of Reason that many claimed had arrived in Europe, a period where Science had overtaken Religion in Man's search for truth. So just as Science was busy explaining the meaning of life in mathematical principles, reducing chaos to order and reason, so too were the great architects of the day reducing their universe to mathematical forms, to models of perfection. Typically this meant that the new buildings, usually of brick or ashlar adhered to precise proportions; the facades, usually of two storeys with an optional attic, would be symmetrical with a central door and windows disposed equally each side of it. The windows on the main floor would be the largest and would be based on the proportions of a double square and would diminish in size with each floor as they neared the roof. The rooms inside would be laid out symmetrically with little regard for comfort or convenience. The roof would be shallow pitched and hidden behind a parapet. There would be little or no decoration, any beauty of form deriving from the sublime proportions of the building. But the wonderful thing about this new style, this way of building, was that it was equally suitable for palace and cottage, all could be brought within its munificent ambit. And with the publication of scale plans and drawings in widely disseminated pattern books, any architect or builder could remain true to its principles. He no longer needed to think, he need merely follow the pattern to produce an acceptable design.

Throughout the eighteenth and well into the nineteenth centuries these same basic principles informed the architecture of England. Within the confines of the rules, fashions came and went, producing a variety of styles but all were to a greater or lesser degree subservient to the rules of proportion. It was inevitable that architecture would react to this constriction in different ways. The best architects, the Adam brothers and Kent and others found ingenious ways to make the style flower while remaining true to its exact principles, while the less able produced a monotonous body of work that, in its dull correctness, depressed the eye.

But gradually, as time went by and it became less necessary to reduce nature to strict rules, the need for individuality began to make itself felt. The Industrial Revolution had produced a climate of entrepreneurial endeavour and the old order held less attraction. With the advent of a fresh young monarch on the throne and British enterprise reaching new heights, it was inevitable that Art would seek to forge ahead with new ideas, not least in the field of architecture. While a reaction to the human arrogance of the Age of Reason gave way in the first years of the nineteenth century to a more romantic, less structured society, so in architecture a reaction to the essential constraints of the Neo-Classical style inevitably produced new styles that mirrored the romance and fancy that had been rigorously denied for the best part of a century and a half. At first this was expressed in playful Gothick and whimsical picturesque styles, the cottage ornée proving a popular form. But growing unseen behind this froth was an altogether more serious, more convincing architecture and one moreover that came complete with its own philosophy; that in fact verged on the religious in its intensity.

In 1834, the young A.W.N. Pugin, a renowned Gothic modeller and son of a French émigré, converted to Catholicism and two years later took his religion and his architecture and combined them into something akin to a crusade. His revolutionary *Contrasts – or a Parallel between the Noble Edifices of the Fourteenth and Fifteenth Centuries and Similar Buildings of the Present Day,* was published in 1836 and *The True Principles of Pointed or Christian Architecture* in 1841. He took English architecture and shook it by the scruff of the neck. No longer would the hated alien architecture of Palladio be tolerated in this country, henceforth Gothic was the only true English architecture. In his two works, Pugin laid down what he saw as the fundamental rules of architectural design. Architecture was not a business but a sacred vocation; Classicism was next to Paganism; the only true Christian architecture was that which had obtained up to the Middle Ages – Gothic. And he went further: what he called fidelity to place and to material meant that buildings should be constructed in the local vernacular style and with the materials readily to hand. In over one hundred buildings, Pugin showed just how sublime Gothic could be.

And such was his astonishing ability and religious zeal that within a few years Neo-Classicism had fallen, not out of use maybe but certainly out of favour, and been replaced with a correct Gothic, and the country's foremost art critic – John Ruskin – was vying with Pugin to produce a complete philosophy that would govern all architectural endeavour. Yet despite being common adherents to the cause, Ruskin was always hostile to Pugin, perhaps because he was trying to prove that Gothic emanated from a Protestant ethic, while Pugin was very much wedded to the Catholic cause.

Ruskin's greatness as a critic, "...lay in his profound understanding of the relationship between art and the society that produces it." He argued that while Classical architecture had enslaved Man's thoughts, Gothic had the ability to free him; that though the architectural result might be imperfect, or as he called it – *Savage* – it would be the product of free will. In his great polemical works, especially *The Stones of Venice* of 1853, Ruskin set out his (they were also Pugin's) principles for Gothic architecture. "1: Never encourage the manufacture of any article not absolutely necessary in the production of which invention has no share. 2: Never demand an exact finish for its own sake, but only for practical or noble end. 3: Never encourage imitation or copying of any kind except for the sake of preserving record of great works." This was *Savageness* and these were the central principles that would guide most architects for the next 60 years. Allied to *Savageness* was *Changefulness*. "It is one of the chief virtues of the Gothic builders, that they never suffered ideas of outside symmetry and consistencies to interfere with the real use and value of what they did... If they wanted a window, they opened one; a room, they added one; a buttress, they built one; utterly regardless of any established conventionalities of external appearance..." Ruskin's changefulness was a reaction against the, at times, extreme inconvenience of the Neo-Classical insistence for symmetry and proportion that always overrode convenience.

Gothic allowed the window to be placed where convenience required, Neo-Classicism demanded that it be placed where proportion dictated. While Gothic built its rooms and erected a shell to cover them, Palladianism built a shell and filled it with rooms. While the one built from the inside out, the other built from the outside in. While in the first, form followed function, in the other, function followed form.

And the underlying message that accompanied both Pugin's and Ruskin's writings was the innate nobility of the craftsman. The medieval craftsman had, they believed, been proud of his creativity and free to interpret his material as he saw fit to the greater beauty of his world. Neo-Classicism had destroyed that freedom by insisting on pattern book exactitude in his work. The myth of the Noble Savage was to touch a diverse assemblage of figures during Victoria's reign – the Druid, the American Indian, as well as the medieval craftsman – and it was this nobility of honest toil and its battle against the hated machine-made artefact that drew another of the founding fathers of nineteenth century architectural thought to the cause – William Morris. While Ruskin had been slowly moving towards a political viewpoint via his architectural musings, eventually shipping up in the proto-Socialism of his *St. Georges Guild*, a sort of Craft-Socialism, Morris was from the very beginning a political animal for whom Socialism, with its respect for the dignity of labour, and the crafts were inextricably entwined and whose ideas verged on communism.

Morris had been born in Walthamstow in 1834 to a wealthy family, his father acquiring a fortune through business speculation which, in 1840, allowed the family to move to a large property in Epping Forest. For the next seven years, until the death of his father, the young Morris was free to roam the forest on his pony, absorbing the beauty of nature and the peace of a countryside little touched by the modern age, an almost medieval existence. The rest of his life was spent in attempting to recreate this idyll of a healthy self-sufficiency, an idyll moreover that should be the right of Everyman and not just the wealthy few.

While at university, Morris read Ruskin's *Stones of Venice*.

The effect, especially of the chapter, *The Nature of Gothic*, was revelatory. Ruskin's argument that a nation's art was a public concern and that, "A decline in artistic standards…was an image of a deep cultural malaise", struck a chord in him and he decided that his future lay in architecture. From Oxford, Morris entered the office of the Diocese architect G.E. Street and was soon immersed in a world of Arts, his friend Burne-Jones introducing him to Gabriel Rossetti. Together they began to design and decorate their own furniture and decorated the Oxford Union Building with their designs. With his marriage in 1858 to Jane Burden, another friend, Philip Webb, designed their house and Morris set to with its decoration. Deciding to build on this decorative experience, Morris, together with some friends founded Morris, Marshall, Fawlkner & Co, producing interior designs and furniture in line with his love of medieval decoration, employing craftsmen in wood, metal and glass to produce a wide range of decorative items from furniture to jewellery and wall-paper in a naturalistic style that provided a link with the halcyon days of his childhood. Morris had established a Crafts-Guild in line with Ruskin's thinking and his energy ensured that it was a commercial success.

Though Morris had quickly realized after his time in Street's office that he had not the slightest flair for architecture, he understood its importance as an art form, seeing it as a "…union of the arts mutually helpful and harmoniously subordinated to one another." He believed that where, "…new buildings must be built, by building them well and in a common sense and unpretentious way, with the good material of the countryside, they will take their place alongside of the old houses and look, like them, a real growth of the soil." These sentiments were *manna* to a rising generation of architects who, though sympathetic to the Gothic tradition, saw in it little room for development; but Morris's hope that "…the new and genuine architecture…" would spring from new buildings in tune with but not copies of the vernacular tradition opened up new horizons and spurred a growth in architecture that brought the world beating a path to England's shores.

Between them, Pugin, Ruskin and Morris, laid the basic principles that would guide English architecture through its finest flowering, not just another style but a complete way of building, that came to be known as Arts and Crafts. Its greatest exponents – Webb, Shaw, Lutyens – built on the vernacular tradition to produce relaxed buildings that melted into the countryside. These works of art were widely visited by other architects who in turn interpreted what they saw in their own style. And central to the Arts and Crafts tradition was a respect for the buildings of the past as a repository of the noble craft of building design. It was for this reason that the heavy and unfeeling restoration of old buildings in the nineteenth century was frowned upon by the Arts and Crafts movement. It was typically Morris who actually did something about it and formed The Society for the Protection of Ancient Buildings – SPAB in 1877.

This halcyon period, from about 1850 to 1900 saw England emerge as the centre of the architectural world and the Arts and Crafts ideal exported to the continent and America. But though founded on egalitarian principles, it contained within it the seeds of its destruction. The Arts and Crafts Movement had hoped to give freedom of expression and creativity to the craftsman; to the mason, carpenter and painter that they might produce their art as they saw fit. But very few architects were prepared to relinquish their hold over design in this way and so the craftsman remained subject to another's whim. It had also hoped that its architecture would be available to everyone, not just the rich; but the hand-crafting that was supposed to give the craftsman his freedom and the avoidance of machine-made materials that was central to the style meant that it was only the wealthy who could afford it. This paradox would ensure that the Arts and Crafts Movement could survive only so long as well-off patrons were able to afford the extravagance that its principles demanded and those patrons, and the philosophy that had underwritten the cause, would disappear almost overnight with the advent of the Great War. Morris had understood this paradox and was greatly vexed by it, berating a patron who had enquired why he appeared upset, "It is only that I spend my life in ministering to the swinish luxury of the rich."

Though the Vernacular Revival had swept all before it in the latter years of the nineteenth century, Neo-Classicism had retained its adherents and now, as the century died, its complex possibilities began to attract others to its cause. Perhaps the most influential of these was Edwin Lutyens – the arch progenitor of the Arts and Crafts ideal. Lutyens was the quintessential Arts and Crafts architect yet he was the first to betray it. A paradox perhaps but the essential point was that Lutyens had never belonged to the Arts and Crafts brotherhood anyway; he was an artist and went wherever the search for perfection took him. Having largely exhausted the possibilities of vernacular, he turned more and more to the classical tradition which, it could be argued, was equally legitimate as a vernacular form, and which offered the possibility of producing complex essays in proportion and geometry, a style that, for Lutyens, had its climax in the building of New Delhi.

As fashion turned from the vernacular to classical forms, those architects who held true to Arts and Crafts ideals and refused to sully themselves saw their practices wither and collapse. The Grand Manner was not for them but others such as Newton and Blomfield found it greatly to their taste, finding the style particularly suited to urban locations which had never really suited vernacular designs; and besides, its use of machine-made materials made it cheaper. And cost, from here on would be, if not the deciding factor, certainly one of the most important.

A confident Great Britain had entered the war in 1914 as one of the premier powers, that confidence backed by its control of half of the globe. By 1918, though its territories remained largely intact, the social upheaval that the conflict had caused had brought about a revolution that touched every aspect of life for its inhabitants. The ungraspable loss of life brought about a fundamental re-evaluation of society and brought about the end of the old order and not only in Britain but all over the continent. The Modern World had arrived; austerity in art and architecture came to the fore with stark, monolithic structures devoid of ornament. The brutality, the ugliness that had endured for four years struck at the heart of art everywhere, producing images that mirrored the savagery, the austerity of war. In architecture, the grey concrete fortifications of the western front became models for the gaunt concrete blocks of flats that became the abiding image of the Brutal style on the continent. In Britain, the worst excesses of the style were avoided, replaced by Modernism which sought to evince a thorough break with the past in its clean, uncluttered lines, its lack of ornament and its use of new materials, in a reaction against prettiness and beauty. In many ways it was just as ugly as the Brutalism of the continent but it thought itself thoroughly modern, even if it did borrow heavily from the great Arts and Crafts architect Voysey.

In a sense, the Modern Movement of the 1920s paved the way for the system building of the sixties and seventies, with its emphasis on urban landscapes, clean unbroken lines and lack of ornament. At first the new building methods and the political energy that propelled them had held the promise of a modern home for everyone. The sixties watchwords – *new* and *modern* – led to a natural expectation that that also meant *better*; what it often meant in practice was *untried* and *untested*; in the sense of how these structures would last over time and how they would effect the communities who had to live in them. Often, the only thing that the new methods and materials - the machine production, the precast concrete, the flat roofs and the large expanses of glazing - had going for them was novelty and cheapness. But the novelty of leaking roofs, massive condensation and unsafe buildings all too quickly faded and the cost of renovation just a few years after construction rapidly took local authority budgets into the red.

So though undeniably modern, these building methods were largely rejected by society once their drawbacks became apparent, only becoming acceptable when clothed in more traditional materials and then under sufferance. With half the architectural profession working for local authorities in the late sixties, Modernism was, after all, "…a mixture of social service and heavy industry." It was not here that man's love affair with architecture was played out but in that great Victorian institution – the Suburb.

The great hope of the Arts and Crafts revolutionaries that their architecture could be shared with the masses did not die after-all. It was pounced upon by every speculative builder in Britain, reinvented, and raised anew in every street in suburbia; tile-hung and weather-boarded in its own little garden. The bow-window, the stained glass, Voysey's gables and rough-cast and Harrison Townsend's Romanesque porches are all there. If they are now devoid of meaning and often applied with little or no understanding of their role, yet this is what Everyman wants, it is his most earnest desire. His dream is not a concrete tower block in an urban jungle, it is a little house in a little garden that dimly remembers its vernacular heritage, hidden behind a mock Tudor facade.

The identification of Modernism with Socialism was never going to survive the discrediting of the Socialist Utopia that finally occurred in 1979 and with the advent of a new style to replace the system building of earlier decades came a problem. What to call it? This new style was not really an urban one, yet neither was it rural or suburban. It was not Modernist but neither was it Neo-Classical and it certainly was not vernacular. Post-Modernism as it came to be called tended to emerge on the edge of urban conurbations and to be the favoured style for offices and industrial complexes. Stylistically, it borrowed from the Neo-Classical to adorn modernist elevations with simplistic chunky porticoes and cornices. It has been likened to designing with children's building blocks and indeed, with its bright primary colours and bold simple shapes, there is a strong resemblance.

In a move away from the sterile uniformity of the seventies and eighties with its bleak and endless curtain walls, the Post-Modern design has become lighter, playful while simultaneously striving for economy and low maintenance costs. Today's architectural philosophy is not about proportion, not about a crafts' utopia but is about reflecting the human condition. Throughout the history of architecture, at least in the last three hundred years, building styles and the philosophies behind them, have reflected the social condition that brought them about. Sometimes it is not possible to see that reflection except with the benefit of hindsight, but as an art form, it is always there; we just cannot always see it.

WEST SURREY ARCHITECTURE

Even a cursory glance at the work of England's best-known architects reveals that Surrey, and West Surrey in particular, is a repository for a substantial part of their work. The reasons for this apparent disparity in distribution are several but principally revolve around the proximity of the area to London and architects' familiarity with the Surrey and Sussex countryside.

The great explosion of architectural commissions in the nineteenth century principally derived from wealthy middle class families seeking houses in the country surrounding the capital; either as occasional retreats from every day life in the metropolis or as permanent homes from which to commute to the capital. The enormous growth in transport links, and particularly the railways, had made both a country house and a business career in London not only possible but desirable. The railway had reached Guildford from London in 1845 and by 1859 connected the coast at Portsmouth with the capital, providing the towns and villages along the route with a speedy and reliable link to London for the first time, a link moreover that was rapidly seized upon by those anxious to enjoy the delights of the country while still chasing money in London.

The nineteenth century cult of the picturesque a romantic, idealized, view of rural life that had grown unbidden as a bulwark against the rapid industrialization of so much in life, was sold to a willing urban audience surrounded by the noisome odours and clamour of modern city life. The heathlands of West Surrey, with their Scots pines and swathes of heather, became useful substitutes for the highly valued landscapes and clean bracing airs of the Scottish Highlands and quickly became popular resorts for the well-to-do. Complete new settlements such as Hindhead and Holmbury St.Mary soon grew up on these previously value-less and "wild" heaths as the new commuting classes established themselves in the country around Haslemere and Farnham, Godalming and Guildford. These were the clients for whom the Gothic Revival and later, the Arts and Crafts architects designed.

And as a thousand year old way of life was squeezed out of the countryside by this invasion, so did the value of the vernacular architecture of the area at last become apparent. While city based architectural students descended on the wealden lanes in search of models for their designs, other students - those native to West Surrey - were joining the vernacular revival with an intimate knowledge of the old ways already learned. Architects such as Lutyens, Woodyer and Falkner had spent their formative years absorbing the traditional ways of construction and had little need of the sketching tours of Surrey and Sussex that were mandatory for the keen pupil. But whether native or immigrant, the lessons learned from the study of old rural buildings were applied with love and respect to many new designs, allowing them to blend successfully into the rural landscape of West Surrey.

And with this intense study came a love for the traditional materials, the great wealden oaks used for the timber framing of cottage and farmhouse and Bargate Stone, a hard calcareous sandstone from the Bargate Beds of the Lower Greensand quarried around Godalming. Local handmade bricks from the many small brickworks on the wealden clay for chimney and hearth and ironstone galletting to strengthen the mortar joints. But the architects were not afraid to experiment with new technology when it presented itself. Thackeray Turner used concrete extensively in one of his Guildford commissions, several other Arts and Crafts architects also trying it out, while Lutyens used both concrete and steel joists in The Red House in Godalming, though was careful to tuck them away out of sight.

Remarkably, given their ease of access by road and rail, the market towns of West Surrey:- Haslemere, Farnham and Godalming, having gathered to themselves a variety of respectable architecture from the nineteenth and early twentieth centuries, were subsequently able to avoid the worst excesses of later twentieth century architecture and town planning. In no small measure this was due to the enlightened leadership of civic amenity groups and

HERITAGE OF WAVERLEY LIMITED

Groton
Ballfield Road
Godalming
Surrey
GU7 2HE

25 April 2002

Mrs P.G. Green
5 Rectory Close.

Dear Mrs Green

West Surrey Architecture 1840-2000:
Pre-Publication Orders

I am pleased to enclose with this letter a copy (or copies) of "West Surrey Architecture 1840-2000" (signed by the Author, Christopher Budgen),which you ordered and paid for in advance of the book's publication. We hope you will enjoy and value it (and maybe recommend it to your friends!).

You may like to know that Heritage of Waverley Ltd—the company set up by the 3 civic societies in Waverley to market the book—intend to publish it on 7 May; and that copies will be on sale in local bookshops from that date.

I should be grateful f you, or the person receiving the book on your behalf, would be good enough to sign the return slip below to acknowkedge receipt.
Yours sincerely

Alan Brown
Director, Heritage of Waverley Ltd

individuals who cared passionately for their towns and were prepared to speak out when these streetscapes were threatened by wholly inappropriate development. Thus today, these three towns offer the visitor a pleasing architectural mixture upon which to rest the eye and if the odd building jolts the sensibilities, the observer may take comfort in the thought that Woking's planning misfortunes were never visited on the settlements of the Western corner of the county.

West Surrey's *modern* architecture (if it can be called that) really began in 1842 with the invitation of Viscount Middleton of Peperharow to the young and terribly influential Augustus Pugin. His brief was to provide a series of buildings for the estate that would add interest to the Viscount's view of his park. The result was a remarkable collection of strict Gothic buildings by one of the foremost architects of his age and before long other renowned architects were being approached to produce designs in a variety of Vernacular Revival styles. Principle among these was Philip Webb and Richard Norman Shaw. Webb's master - G.E. Street - had built himself a house on the outskirts of Ewhurst at Holmbury St.Mary and designed and paid for a church for the fledgling settlement, and soon Webb was producing designs for houses in the hills round about. Shaw was also busy, especially around Haslemere and produced several buildings in the town and its offspring Hindhead as well as a massive new bank for Farnham in an Elizabethan style that sadly did not survive the *Georgification* of the town under Harold Falkner, one of its saviours. Falkner spent almost his entire professional career working in the vicinity of his birthplace and Farnham can boast over one hundred buildings designed by this remarkable man who took neo-Georgian to his heart and almost rebuilt his home town.

As these architects' work in the area became known to the next wave of architectural students, they became places of pilgrimage, essential stop-overs on the endless sketching tours and thus another generation fell under the spell of West Surrey's quiet charm. But its most famous product in the field of architecture had no need of pilgrimage – he was already there; in Thursley where he was raised from an early age. It sometimes seems that Lutyens did not have an early life or pupilage like other people; that with a flash of lightning and a clap of thunder, he stepped from the pages of history ready formed as the most capable, most versatile architect of the age. Of course it was not quite like that. But his childhood in Thursley and the country lanes of West Surrey had given him ample time to absorb the intricacies of the local vernacular and the mysteries of carpentry and brickwork. His subsequent mastery of whichever style was required and his later triumph in the raising of New Delhi were all built on the foundation of the rural building craft of West Surrey.

Another local lad to influence his chosen field was Henry Woodyer, a Guildford boy. His work was mainly concerned with ecclesiastical architecture. Building on the work of George Gilbert Scott and other early Gothic Revival architects, Woodyer produced a body of work in the area that showed a much more intense understanding of what could be achieved in a religious structure. His churches at Grafham and Hascombe were models of highly decorative design that were much favoured by the High Church advocates of the day and certainly met with the approval of the Ecclesiastical Society.

At the nether end of the nineteenth century came two architects for whose designs there appear to be no likely pigeon-holes. In a loose sense they were both deeply influenced by the vernacular revival and the principles of the Arts and Crafts movement but as their careers developed, their designs became much more individual and difficult to categorize. As the century closed and Neo-Classical became the style that everyone wanted, these two architects, firm in their detestation of the classical medium and unable to bring themselves to use it, saw there practices shrink and almost collapse. Charles Voysey was a Yorkshireman but after serving his articles, latterly with George Devey, he began to produce designs which were stripped down versions of the more traditional Arts and Crafts models. His lifelong striving for simplicity in his designs meant that his work was very different from the more traditional work of his contemporaries, and striking in its differences.

Charles Harrison Townsend was another Arts and Crafts adherent and early member of the Art Worker's Guild. His best-known designs were for galleries and museums in London in an exuberant Arts and Crafts style that bordered on the Baroque and who later produced a sizeable body of work in another fledgling settlement on the heath at Blackheath. Like Voysey, his individual designs are striking, many incorporating the Romanesque arch at the principle entrance.

But the sundering of tradition (one might almost say of all tradition) that resulted from the Great War meant that the conditions and the social environment that had brought forth these architectural gems ceased to exist almost overnight. It is true that pale copies could still be found in the 1920s but the march of the Modernists swept all before it. Or did it?

What actually tended to occur in West Surrey, was that new building design slipped back into a vague Neo-Georgian, evident in the schools of the County Architects Department for Surrey County Council; or a completely stripped vernacular style for local authority housing projects. While these designs were providing badly needed buildings for the area, they were not great architecture (and indeed some might argue that such a thing had ceased to exist anyway), and it was not until the sixties that sufficient confidence (and government funding) meant that radical new designs began to make their appearance in West Surrey. By and large it was the County Architects Department that led the way with system built designs for schools, health centres and police stations such as its 1968 design for Godalming Police Station in precast concrete and dark brick, an unloved design now under threat of demolition. In the private sector, unfortunate modern additions to older buildings (such as the Branksome Conference Centre at Haslemere) did nothing to foster a greater acceptance of machine production and it was only when stark concrete was disguised with more traditional brick cladding, as at Charterhouse, that modern buildings could be accepted into the local environment.

The disappointments of architecture as a social service and its cynical use as a vote catcher, "…470,000 new flats and houses completed in 1967…", meant that by the early 1970s production line architecture was doomed. Its radical excursions into new ways of building and designing guaranteed that what followed would be its exact opposite – bland pastiches that tried hard not to upset anybody. West Surrey's towns took their fair share of these designs; vaguely vernacular, vaguely classical, instantly forgettable, and it was not until the nineties that post modern elements began to make their appearance in the streets of West Surrey, normally as replacements for those radical sixties designs. Those, after all were often the only buildings in the towns that the inhabitants were prepared to give up without a fight.

And because the town centres are populated by buildings replete with history, any new designs tend to be grouped about the towns' nether regions; the Millennium Centre in Farnham being a typical example. This spirited design by John Monk in Crosby Way, completed in 1999 typifies both the location and the style of much that is Post Modern. But if the style has a failing, it is that it is essentially urban, it has yet to find a face that will be tolerated in Surrey's leafy lanes, but it will, in time.

Augustus Welby Northmore Pugin

1812 - 1852

Augustus Welby Northmore Pugin

1812 - 1852

"We should have had no Morris, no Street, no Burges, no Shaw, no Webb, no Bodley, no Rossetti, no Burne-Jones, no Crane, but for Pugin." John Dando Sedding, 1888.

Sedding was not being merely polite when he heaped such honour on A.W.N. Pugin. It is fair to say that Pugin was the foremost architectural thinker of his day, a man who took an entire architectural style and made it his own, but more than that – he made others wonder why it was that they had ever used any other style.

His father A.C. Pugin had studied at the Royal Academy and had fled France during the Revolution to set up in England assisting architects including Nash by providing accurate Gothic detailing for fashionably picturesque country houses. His precocious son Augustus was soon imbued with the intricacies of Gothic design and was quickly recognized as the more knowledgeable of the two. The father produced a number of publications on Gothic architecture aided by his son who, such was his reputation by this time as *the* expert in his field that, by his teens was designing the furniture for Sir Jeffrey Wyattville's Windsor Castle and the decorative details for Barry's Houses of Parliament.

By his late teens, Pugin was running the family business providing architects with architectural detailing – anything which could be executed remotely and attached to the building later. Although he more or less held a monopoly – few others could execute Gothic work with his flair after such a long reign of Classical architecture – the business failed in 1831: architect extraordinaire, but no businessman.

In 1834, Pugin converted to Catholicism; an event that seemed to presage a sea change in his life. If he had been unsure of the path that his life should take (and there is nothing to suggest that he was) any uncertainty was now swept aside. In 1836 and still only 25, his momentous book *"Contrasts – or a Parallel between the Noble Edifices of the Fourteenth and Fifteenth Centuries and Similar Buildings of the Present Day"*, was published. In it, Pugin began to lay down the fundamental laws of English Architecture as he saw them. Firstly, architecture was not merely a business but a sacred calling. Secondly, Classicism was for him the architecture of Paganism. The only true Christian architecture was that which had obtained up to the Middle Ages – Gothic. *Contrasts* compared the present day Classical architecture with Gothic pre-Reformation England and found it wanting: the noble craft of old had been displaced by a mean utilitarian international style, that had no place in England. For Pugin, "Catholic England was merry England, at least for the humble classes."

In his next book *The True Principles of Pointed or Christian Architecture* of 1841, Pugin applied himself more closely to the Gothic cause with more exact design principles. "The two great rules for design are these: First, that there should be no features about a building which are not necessary for convenience, construction or propriety; second, that all ornament should consist of the essential construction of the building. The neglect of these two rules is the cause of all the bad architecture of the present time." To these could be added the fact that "a building and everything in it should be honest reflections of materials as well as of functions": the materials used in construction should not pretend to be something else; and "fidelity to place": a building should be made of the traditional, locally available materials. It was these principles that were to shape and guide architecture for the next sixty years and upon which an entirely new branch of architecture would be based.

But it was not merely his religious proclivities that turned Pugin against the predominant Classicism, ("a bastard Greek") which he correctly identified as an alien style (at least to England), it was simply that Gothic was a more rational and sensible style. The demand for symmetry that Classicism imposed meant that the architect was always

The Gatehouse, Oxenford Grange

trying to shoehorn different functions into a rigid shell. He drew a contrast between the two by pointing out that, for the architect faced with the problem of housing different functions in one building, "the great difference between the principles of Classic and Pointed domestic architecture...(were that) in the former he would be compelled to devise expedients to conceal these irregularities; in the latter he has only to beautify them."

Although Pugin's great desire was to build churches (and most of his buildings were), he accepted commissions for other buildings such as Alton Towers in Staffordshire for Lord Shrewsbury, work on Henry Drummond's house and the nearby church at Albury and for Viscount Midleton at Peperharow. Indeed he was responsible for at least one hundred buildings in his short life including two for himself, but his strict adherence to principle and his manic dedication to the cause of architecture led to many struggles with his patrons.

This mania had, by the time he was forty, overtaken him and he died in 1852, partly no doubt through overwork. Pugin's reputed reply, when asked why he did not employ a clerk to assist with the more mechanical parts of his working drawings had been, "Clerk, my dear Sir, clerk, I never employ one; I should kill him in a week."

He had always encouraged students of architecture to travel the country, the better to understand the various regional styles that made up traditional English design. After his death a memorial fund organized by his colleagues raised over £1000 which RIBA used to establish the Pugin Travelling Scholarship to finance student's travel within England. Ironically the pure form of Gothic that Pugin had preached outlived him by less than a year. Architecture moved on to other forms; but the guiding principles that he

St. Nicholas Church, Peperharow

had laid down: conviction and sincerity, propriety and truth to materials, were taken up by a new generation of architects and became the foundation for what would become known as The Arts and Crafts Movement.

In 1843 Pugin had come to Peperharow at the instigation of the fifth Viscount Midleton; the house and estate near Godalming having been developed by the third and fourth Viscounts in the second half of the 18th century. The fine house, complete in 1765, had been designed by Sir William Chambers in a Classical style; what Nairn & Pevsner described as "careful Academism", with a porch of Portland stone by C.R. Cockerell added in the year of Pugin's arrival. The presence of the arch-critic of Classicism and one of its fiercest adherents on the same site must have brought forth some interesting discussions; one wonders if efforts were made to ensure that the two did not meet.

Pugin however was not there to work on the house but to improve the estate. The next two years were spent adding a series of pure Gothic buildings to the farm at Oxenford Grange on the southern boundary of the park. These comprised a barn, granary and other farm buildings, a gatehouse and a folly containing the Bonneville spring, grouped around the original farmhouse. All of the new buildings closely adhered to Pugin's strict architectural principles, being designed in what we would now recognize as Early English - a style that Pugin thought particularly suitable for remote and therefore primitive areas - and this lends the assemblage an air of timelessness, giving the appearance of the remains of some medieval religious establishment; an outpost perhaps of nearby Waverley Abbey. Indeed, this was precisely the impression for which Pugin was aiming. There is reason to believe – and it was accepted as fact at the time – that Oxenford Grange was a former holding of nearby Waverley Abbey. George Broderick, writing in 1880 noted that, "The new farm buildings close by the gatehouse represent Mr. Pugin's idea of the barns and sheds appropriate to a conventual farm." At the same time that he was overseeing the work here, he was also building his second house – The Grange – for himself at Ramsgate, as well as continuing work on the remodelling

The Great Barn, Oxenford Grange

of Scarisbrick Hall in Lancashire.

Unlike some of his other commissions where it would appear that the patron's wishes caused Pugin to dilute his strong views, at Oxenford Grange he was apparently given a free hand to design a complementary range of buildings reflecting his architectural philosophy and unshakable faith in the cause of Gothic. There is no accommodation here, no Gothic detail tacked on to a later building - this is pure Early English architecture at its best. The complete range is heavily buttressed and built in warm Bargate stone cut small and laid regularly almost like brickwork, with ashlar dressings, the barn and farm buildings forming an open quadrangle around the yard with the gatehouse behind to the west.

The great barn, of six bays, so reminiscent of the stone tithe barns of the monastic orders overlooks the farm pond. Stone gables with the minimum of decoration top walls with narrow window slits. Central in each of the long sides is a gabled entrance which on the yard side, is flanked by tiled roofed lean-tos, one stone walled and the other formerly open sided (though presently filled with cement block walling). Within the barn the window splays and door angles have been quoined in moulded brick rather than ashlar work and the roof is of unusual design. High up on the walls corbels support massive arched braces which continue upwards and across the roof space to meet the opposite purlin, thus forming sets of cross braces down the roof while in the entrance gables a corbel table just under the eaves line supports these subsidiary roofs. The whole affair is unusual and entirely unexpected in a rural building not least because this must be one of very few stone farm buildings in West Surrey.

The gatehouse to the west is again gabled with large arches fore and aft giving access to the farm. Between the arches the vaulted space contains a pair of massive studded gates closing off the entrance, the central boss of the vault carved to represent the Ox from which the farm was named while the front wall below the windows carries the arms of the Midleton family. Nairn and Pevsner believed that the barn and gatehouse were "…among his best buildings, a proof that for him, at least some of the time, medieval architecture was not simply an –*ism* but a complete method of design."

Behind the farmhouse lay ruins of a building believed to be the former Peperharow house, part of which includes a wall containing a three light lancet window which is almost identical to that in the east wall of the chancel of the church close by and attributed to Pugin. Did he copy this window for his chancel or did he rearrange the ruins to form a more picturesque grouping, strictly against his code?

The following year Pugin turned to the Norman Church of St. Nicholas lying in a peaceful setting within the park and more or less rebuilt it. The south wall of the nave and the doorway are almost all that remain of the original Norman church while the tower is later, 1826. Pugin was responsible for the Romanesque chancel arch and the north aisle and most of the decorative work within the church. His ornate chancel arch is stark and crisp with Norman moulding forming a dominant feature and contrasts with his Early English work on the north aisle and the Decorated chancel. In this way Pugin was able to produce a design that appeared to have evolved through the ages but which was still in harmony with the remaining Norman work and with its rural surroundings.

Pugin then was one of England's foremost architectural thinkers and had a profound effect on his period. Peperharow stands as a monument both to Pugin and to Gothicism.

Pugin's Buildings:

The Great Barn, Oxenford Grange, Milford, Witley. 1843

Granary and Farm Buildings, Oxenford Grange, Milford, Witley. 1843

Gate House, Oxenford Grange, Milford, Witley. 1843-4

Bonneville Spring Folly, Elstead, Witley. 1843

Church of St. Nicholas, Peperharow. 1844

Henry Woodyer

1816 - 1896

Henry Woodyer

1816 - 1896

"...an architect who has profited by antiquarian study – not...an antiquary who has tried his hand at architecture."
C.L. Eastlake, 1872

In his *History of the Gothic Revival* of 1872, Eastlake had sought to record the salient facts of the revival in Gothic architecture that had sprung from Pugin's pioneering work. In singling out Woodyer as an exemplar of the style, he was highlighting the work of an architect who had consistently eschewed publicity, believing it, and the persona of the country Gentleman, to be mutually exclusive. Because of this, Woodyer, although his work is locally abundant, has suffered an undeserved obscurity so that large chunks of his life are unknown.

Caleb Woodyer, a member of the Company of Surgeons, ran a successful practice in Guildford High Street. Married to Mary Anne Halsey in 1808, the couple had two daughters and then a son – Henry. Fortune favoured the Woodyers and the family's wealth was used to ensure a good education for the boy, and at 13, Henry was sent to Eton. Here Woodyer formed the friendships and links with the country's influential families that were to sustain him in his later career.

After Eton, Woodyer moved to Merton College, Oxford and into the heart of Victorian religious radicalism. It was here that the attempts to bring the Church of England nearer to the Church of Rome, at least doctrinally, were most intense. Out of this ferment rose the Oxford Movement (or Tractarianism) led by Keble, Pusey and John Henry Newman and its resulting High Church ideals were strongly embraced by the young Woodyer who later joined The Ecclesiological Society, another Romanist group, though more concerned with the artistic ideals of Christianity and thus more suited to Woodyer's artistic leanings. But although Woodyer was certainly in thrall of the Church and its mystique, while still at Merton he was already being labelled Bohemian and developing that certain eccentricity that appeared

indispensable to any claiming an artistic inclination.

As the time approached to leave Oxford in 1838, Woodyer had little idea of a future career and indeed, as his friend Parry said many years later, "...(architecture) was the last profession he thought of, he never dreamt he was fit for it..." While the church no doubt exerted its pull, he felt that, strong sympathies notwithstanding, it was not for him; he had a certain position to maintain. But gradually, his mind settled on the art (as opposed to the craft) of architecture yet, to maintain what he considered to be his social status, he was always careful (more so in later life) not to publicize his work or to pursue it as a profession; he was, after all, a Gentleman. But while this distancing from the nitty-gritty of the profession satisfied his social station, it did little to endear him to others of a similar calling so that, throughout his career, there were few architects that he could call friends.

It is entirely consistent with Woodyer's life that one of those few with whom he could legitimately claim friendship was William Butterfield. Like Woodyer, he shied away from publicity but was none the less much sought after, particularly for ecclesiastical commissions. His work was often bold and imaginative, sometimes quirky but always worth study, and it was probably to Butterfield and no one else that Woodyer turned when his decision to practise architecture had been formed. Woodyer's chosen calling, however it was dressed up, was not a likely choice for the Eton and Oxford educated son of a wealthy surgeon. It may be that links within the family had some bearing on his decision. His aunt, for example, had married the Rector of Peperharow and their son William had married Elizabeth, Woodyer's sister in 1842. Peperharow was of course host to Pugin for much of the 1840s as he carried out commissions

Cranleigh School

for Viscount Midleton on the estate and church and indeed Pugin had Woodyer's name and address in his diary in 1845.

However it came about, it seems likely that at some point in the early 1840s Woodyer did enter Butterfield's office in some capacity though, given his education and the closeness of their ages, not under conventional articles. By 1846 Woodyer appears in the London street directories as an architect living and working at Adam Street, Adelphi and the following year both worked on the church at Ottery St Mary. Yet, however Woodyer gained his architectural training, whether by formal or informal means, he demonstrated a competent ability that soon flowered into a style not unlike Butterfield's – the quirkiness, the imagination, which, given the religious nature of most of their commissions, was not always easy to demonstrate.

Woodyer's family connections were in play early in his career (as was often the case, many architects first commissions were obtained through such links). Woodyer's elder sister had married Lannoy Coussmaker, Lord of the Manor of Wyke, just outside Guildford and it was here in 1844 that he designed his first church in the correct Middle-Pointed or Decorated style; (with Pugin a short distance away, there was perhaps a desire to "get it right"). But his first commission had in fact been the restoration of an earlier church – Alfold, obtained through his brother-in-law at Peperharow. The restoration of country churches would become a staple of his work throughout his career and one for which later generations would berate him and other restorers for the history that they swept away. In their defence, if one is needed, (and it certainly wasn't then) many of these buildings were in a parlous condition; poorly maintained, ill lit and hardly altered since their construction in medieval times. While the loss of this historical record jars with our conserving sentiments, for Woodyer and his colleagues, these were still living buildings, but failing to meet the needs of a vigorous church-going society.

By the age of 35, Woodyer was well on the way to being an established architect. He had a respectable number of commissions under his belt and had opened an office in

Church of St Andrew, Grafham

Guildford. In August 1851 he married Frances, daughter of J.S. Bowles, Woodyer's contemporary at Eton and Oxford and had purchased an estate at Grafham in Bramley on which to build a house for his rapidly approaching family. Ironically, the years prior to his marriage were probably Woodyer's happiest and most fulfilling. He and Frances were engaged and from another contemporary from his Eton days he obtained a commission to build a new church at Highnam, Gloucester. This was Gambier Parry, his school friend, whose wife had died in childbirth (a coincidence of which Woodyer was, as yet, unaware) and the church was to be his memorial to her and to their other children who had died in infancy. Woodyer poured his artistic endeavours into the work, producing a lasting monument not only to Isabella Parry but to his own creativity.

This work can have been but lately complete when, less than a year into their marriage, Frances died in childbirth. His daughter - his "chick" - survived and was christened Hester. Having buried Frances at the family estate at Milton, Woodyer returned to Grafham, to grieve, to recover.

Work meanwhile continued at Grafham in turning the existing house into a suitable country residence and by 1854, Grafham Grange was largely complete. Throughout the 1850s Woodyer produced a series of buildings around the country, often for charitable organizations and often refusing payment. In 1860, having given up his office in London some years previously, his mind turned to Grafham once more which he shared with Hester and his widowed mother, and here he produced a series of buildings for the hamlet starting with a chapel as a memorial to his wife. St. Andrew's shows Woodyer's abilities - at their best when designing a small building – in total control of the material. Bargate stone has been used, cut small and laid regularly, but with moulded brick dressings. Substantial buttresses support the nave and chancel walls and a rustic porch of massy timbers provides a counterpoint to the slender, airy spire topping the shingled bell-cote over the west gable. Inside, the semi-circular apse is used to good effect in focussing the eye on the altar area with carved and painted decoration while over the sedilia are carved busts of himself and Frances and between them a nest containing their chick. Later he also

Church of St Peter, Hascombe

designed the school next door and a nearby farmhouse.

Although Woodyer had started out in the 1840s as a broad adherent of Pugin's strict principles and was recognized by Eastlake and others as a Gothicist, his later work became more individual and imaginative, as Quiney correctly noted, this was expressed in the detail rather than the plan or massing of his designs. This was more particularly evident in the commissions for new buildings, for example at Hascombe and Grafham, rather than the numerous restorations that he accepted. St. Peter's, Hascombe, was a small church, probably of Saxon origin, largely demolished and rebuilt in 1864. It was here that Woodyer, the Tractarian Architect met Musgrave, the High Church Patriarch. Vernon Musgrave had been inducted as Rector of Hascombe in 1862. A man of exceptional drive and vision, he immediately set about bringing the parish into the 19th century, his first target being the parish church. This small building, now believed to have been a largely Saxon construction, fell far short of Musgrave's expectations; apart from anything else, it was falling apart and "...the House of

God could not alone remain in its unworthy condition, while wealth and luxury were increasing all round."

With the blessing of the church authorities, the old building was demolished and Woodyer's design, loosely based on the original begun. The new structure was an evolved version of his earlier chapel at Grafham but on a larger scale. Outside, Woodyer kept the design simple (perhaps in recognition of its late antecedent) in Early English, even replacing the apsidal end to the chancel of the earlier church. The material used was Bargate stone with galletted joints lit by a series of double lancets and topped by a bell turret finished with a slender shingled spire. But inside, the richness of the fabric and the originality of the chancel decoration are shockingly different in a country church.

With Woodyer providing the canvas and the basic decorative design, and his client Musgrave, the ardent High Church advocate choosing the palette, the result was always going to be exuberant and the completed design did not disappoint. The nave windows commemorate the life and works of the church's patron saint – St Peter – in stained glass while the painted walls depict the disciples fishing, "…the post-Resurrection miracle of the Apostolic net, with its "hundred and fifty and three" fishes, the exact number on the walls…" The chancel screen - Woodyer had been able to save the original and incorporate it into his new design despite Low Church dislike of such things - fronts a chancel simply filled with decoration. Every surface - walls, windows, roof, even the chancel arch - is used "…to set forth the Angelic Presence…" of the Apostolic creed in paint, glass and sculpture. This remarkable achievement of Victorian ecclesiastical decoration contrasts strongly with Woodyer's work at other churches in the locality where the Low Church, almost Presbyterian, sentiments of the incumbent prevented Woodyer's artistic abilities from manifesting themselves.

At around the same time Woodyer was also at work in Cranleigh on the design for the new Surrey County School (later Cranleigh School), a fee-paying institution for the sons of the middle classes. Here he produced a design in red brick with Mansfield stone dressings and diaper work based around a quadrangle fronted by an imposing chapel all set on rising ground and overlooking the school's playing fields. This extremely attractive design featured several of Woodyer's favourite details, the use of massed dormer windows breaking through the roof line, a series of twin lancets and the chapel with apsidal end.

Also at Cranleigh, Woodyer spent many years working on the restoration of St Nicolas church for the Rector, the Archdeacon Sapte. This was in fact the second restoration that the church had succumbed to, the chancel receiving the attentions of an unknown hand in 1845. The effect of this extensive work on the internal fabric has been to purge it of most of its historical vestiges, leaving a structure clean and worthy but without the archaeological residues or architectural flashes that help make such a building interesting. Compared to his work at Hascombe, which proceeded in tandem with Cranleigh, his work at St Nicolas is almost devoid of decoration. Of more interest is the Rectory that he built for Sapte behind the church to replace an eighteenth century building. Here in a moment of genius, the site chosen was a moated island in the Rectory grounds upon which had stood a very early building, contemporary with the earliest phase of the church. The result is a structure that owes much to Butterfield's Vicarage at Coalpit Heath, Gloucester and Milton Ernest Hall, Bedfordshire; a restrained Gothic in warm brick with sandstone dressings.

Hester was to stay with her father at Grafham until she was in her forties but in 1891 she married a soldier, his subsequent commissions taking them away from England. Woodyer, now alone and with his practice in serious decline, left Grafham to move to Padworth in Berkshire and it was here in 1896 that he died. His body was returned to Grafham and laid to rest beneath the churchyard cross that bore his wife's name yet, with her buried at Milton, they were destined to remain separated even in death.

Woodyer's Buildings:

Church of St. Nicholas, Alfold. Restoration, additions and fittings. 1845-6

Church of St. Peter, Hambledon. 1847

Cosford House, Thursley. Additions. c.1848

Grafham Grange, Grafham. 1854

Grafham Farm, Grafham. 1859

Church of St. John, Milford. 1859

Church of St. Andrew, Grafham. 1860-1

Church of St. Nicolas, Cranleigh. Restoration and additions. 1861-8

Vicarage, Grafham. 1863

Rectory, Cranleigh. 1863

Surrey County School (Cranleigh School). 1863-5

Church of St. Peter, Hascombe. 1863-4

Hascombe School, Hascombe. 1868

Mousehill House, Milford. Additions. 1868-9

Church of St. Mary, Chiddingfold. Restoration, additions and fittings. 1869-70

Grafham School, Grafham. 1871

Church of the Holy Trinity, Bramley. Additions. 1875-6

Church of St. James, Farnham. 1876-77

St. James Church School, Farnham. 1878

Church of St. Andrew, Farnham. Additions. 1881

Church of St. Mary and All Saints, Dunsfold. Restoration. 1882, 1890

Church of St. John the Baptist, Wonersh. Restoration.

Arthur William Blomfield

1829 - 1899

Reginald Theodore Blomfield

1856 - 1942

Arthur William Blomfield
1829 - 1899

Reginald Theodore Blomfield
1856 - 1942

"...the sense of proportion between architecture and the crafts has been lost;
the architectural sense, the power of putting all these beautiful things together and into their right relation,
has disappeared under a prolific growth of cheap accomplishment."
Reginald Theodore Blomfield 1908

Arthur Blomfield was born at Fulham Palace, London in 1829, the son of the Bishop of London. One of the leading Gothic Revival architects of his day, he had been articled to Philip Hardwick and was much sought after by the Church of England clergy for designs for churches, schools and additions and restorations to existing buildings. Indeed almost all of his work was concerned with the church or places of learning in one form or another. Unlike his nephew Reginald, who was widely considered to be cantankerous, Arthur was, "the most delightful of men, witty and cheerful, a first rate amateur actor and a skilful painter in watercolours." His office was a model of relaxed endeavour, somewhat to the chagrin of Reginald who, having expected to find himself, "...in an atmosphere of high ideals, a modern version of the schools or studios of the Italian Renaissance", found instead a cheerful staff much more interested, "...in the latest news, sporting or otherwise, than in the latest experiment in architecture." One of Arthur's pupils in the 1860s was a young Thomas Hardy who, because all design work was dealt with by Blomfield himself – leaving the rather dull tracing to his pupils – eventually left in 1867 to pursue a rather more literary career.

Blomfield's work in Surrey ranged from additions to the new church at Albury in 1868, creating a new apse and transepts, to Merrow and Holy Trinity, Guildford where he added a new chancel and apse in 1888. In 1885, at Charterhouse School, Godalming, (a design by his old master Hardwick), he designed the Great Hall in a light Gothic and the following year, a bridge across Charterhouse Road to connect the school and nearby lodgings, in a similar style. Arthur was knighted in 1889 and awarded the RIBA Gold Medal two years later.

Educated at Haileybury and Oxford, Arthur's nephew Reginald entered his uncle's office in 1881, already a rather opinionated young man. One suspects that even then his ambition and lack of modesty would have made him difficult to get along with. He immediately noted the relaxed atmosphere of the office, not quite to his liking, "I found myself in the company of a somewhat depressed managing clerk, two or three assistants and half a dozen cheerful young fellows who were serving their articles as pupils..." The following year he also became a student at the Royal Academy Schools under Phené Spiers – a product of the Ecole des Beaux Arts – who was soon writing to his father that, "He is so quick and so hard a worker...", and it was true. Reginald was always out on scrambles, sketching the vernacular designs of the southern counties and in 1883 he left the office to tour the continent, sketching in France and Italy where he was most impressed by the Romanesque architecture, a style he considered preferable to Gothic, displaying as it did a more "masculine directness." This preference for the classical form, though nascent at this stage of his career, would later, when the time was right and the climate more tolerant, burst forth and take over his designs.

Not long after his return from the continent Blomfield left his uncle's office to set up practice at an address in Bloomsbury

The Great Hall, Charterhouse

that was also used by E.S. Prior and through him, Blomfield came to meet the group of young architects who had gravitated to Shaw including Letherby and Newton. By 1885 Blomfield had been accepted as a member both of the unofficial Shaw family and the official Art Workers Guild. He quickly absorbed the fundamentals of Shaw's designs and became heavily involved in the Arts and Crafts culture, becoming Hon. Secretary of the Art Workers Guild in 1892 and was also involved with the Arts and Crafts Exhibition Society. In 1889, with others, he became a member of Kenton & Co – a manufacturing concern producing Arts and Crafts inspired furniture – until its demise three years later.

From the earliest days of his professional career then, Blomfield had been heavily immersed in the craft milieu that guided architectural thought at the end of the century. But from then on, as vernacular styles were pushed aside by the return of Classicism, Blomfield was one of the architects who steadily renounced the crafts and concentrated exclusively on neo-Classical design. But for him, it was not enough that the new style, his chosen style, had eclipsed the

old, the entire Arts and Crafts ideal had also to be rejected and in several of his books he took the opportunity to dismiss the philosophy of the Art Workers Guild, William Morris and the whole notion of "The Crafts" as, "…a prolific growth of cheap accomplishments." In this of course, he was following the wisdom of his mentor Shaw who was also not averse to denigrating Morris for the contradictions in his commercial and political life.

Much of Blomfield's practice came after the publication of his books, *A History of Renaissance Architecture in England* in 1897, a shorter version published in 1900 and his book on gardens, *The Formal Garden in England* in 1892. He also produced books on French Renaissance Architecture and a biography of Shaw. These books allowed potential clients to see the possibilities available to them if they chose to build in the new style, and coincidentally provided Blomfield with a lucrative career.

Whatever the Arts and Crafts adherents thought of him, and it wasn't much, Blomfield was influential in the Classical

Wyphurst, Cranleigh

Revival of the early years of the twentieth century. Muthesius referred to him as one of "certain other outstanding domestic Architects entirely on the side of classicising historicism." One of his more interesting and complex designs was for additions to Wyphurst at Cranleigh in 1907-9 where a previous farmhouse had already had additions in the Shaw manner, all gables and tile hanging in the late nineteenth century. Blomfield was tasked with enlarging the house with the addition of a substantial new wing in a vague Tudor style, its red brick facades enlivened with diapering and stone dressings contrasting with the older timbered and tile-hung work. This is especially noticeable on the entrance front where a fine central red brick tower divides timber and tile on the right from red brick and stone on the left. While this dichotomy might have failed in the hands of a lesser architect, Blomfield was able to succeed by keeping the roofs on each side of the tower at the same level and using the Tudor chimney design on both elevations. The garden elevation has no older work, being an almost symmetrical Tudor design centred on a polygonal full height bay, the façade being stopped at each end by further bays this time square. As on the entrance façade, the light stone dressings form an attractive contrast to the deep red diapered brickwork. Altogether an attractive but complex grouping representing an accretive design not often found in the area.

Blomfields' Buildings:

The Great Hall, Charterhouse, Godalming. 1885

Bridge, Charterhouse, Godalming. 1886

Wyphurst, Cranleigh. 1907

The Scott Dynasty

Sir George Gilbert Scott.
1811 - 1878

George Gilbert Scott jun.
1839 - 1897

Sir Giles Gilbert Scott.
1880 - 1960

Richard Gilbert Scott.
1923 -

"The busiest designers were also the busiest restorers, and the busiest of all was George Gilbert Scott."
Roger Dixon & Stephen Muthesius 1978

Scott was considered in his own age to be first and foremost a church architect and it was ecclesiastical architecture that formed the bulk of his practice. But his new designs were at least equalled by his restorations of existing buildings. That he was successful is evident from the commissions that his office attracted, whether he was able to produce works of art in his chosen profession is perhaps open to question. Sir George Gilbert Scott, though coming from humble stock rose to lead the greatest architectural office in Great Britain in the nineteenth century. He made the Gothic Revival his own, taking Pugin's and Ruskin's ideas and transforming them into a form of architecture that could be used to design everything from small country church to major metropolitan landmark.

Born in 1811, the son of a clergyman, as a young man he spent time in a number of offices including those of the London builders Peto and Grissell and the architect Henry Roberts. His studies complete, he set up practice in 1835 with W.B. Moffatt (they stayed together until 1846), and was soon producing designs for churches, workhouses and the like. His first major commission came in 1842 for the church of St Giles in Camberwell, London. In his early work especially, Scott followed Pugin's strictures to keep the design faithful, not to add needless decoration, "fidelity to place, fidelity to materials." Scott's church designs rely on sturdiness, solidity and simplicity for their effect, on buttresses and ample towers; at times this can lead to a stolid worthiness, but at others can rise above the merely workmanlike.

As well as new build designs, Scott carried out hundreds of church and cathedral restorations for which subsequent ages have berated him, perhaps unfairly, but even in his own day the subject was contentious; it was, after-all Morris's horror at Scott's proposals for the restoration of Tewkesbury Cathedral that spawned the birth of the Society for the Protection of Ancient Buildings, which attracted many of his contemporaries to the cause. Morris had written to The Athenaeum noting that, "…it is nothing less than the minster of Tewksbury that is to be destroyed by Sir Gilbert Scott." His immediate wish was that, "…an association be set on foot to keep watch on old monuments, to protest against all "restoration" that means more than keeping out wind and weather…"

But despite the distaste that his restorative measures occasioned among the young SPAB disciples, Scott had hit the mother lode of the Gothic revival and was able to build the most successful architectural practice of his time, the sheer weight of work passing through his office making it impossible for him to be involved in the detail work of every commission, apocryphal stories abounding of Scott's ignorance of just which buildings he was responsible for. But for just this reason, his assistants were given perhaps more freedom than most in their work and therefore went on to become outstanding architects in their own right, those passing through including G.E. Street, Ralph Nevill and G.F. Bodley as well as his sons George and John. Yet despite being the very epitome of the Gothic Revival, Scott, like Shaw later, was happy to produce a Classical design when the situation dictated, such as his design for the Foreign

Church of St Mary, Shackleford

Office. Other prestigious commissions won by his office were the St Pancras Station and Midland Grand Hotel, The Albert Memorial, The Marytrs' Memorial at Oxford and Edinburgh Cathedral.

His work in West Surrey was slight, the church at Farncombe and the church of St Mary at Shackleford, some design work on Godalming church later undertaken by Nevill. The Farncombe design did not impress Nairn & Pevsner who thought it dull but Shackleford did win praise for its proportions especially around the tower though the interior was considered "grim but mechanical."

At his death there were over sixty new buildings or alterations still on the books, the residue of a career covering almost one thousand commissions. His abilities had been recognized in his lifetime, a knighthood being conferred in 1872 and the RIBA Presidency in 1873-5. If nothing else

Scott had shown how Gothic could be successfully integrated into both urban and rural landscapes, producing functional buildings which, though not always works of art, were at least an alternative to neo- Classicism.

George's eldest son George had a short and tragic career curtailed by psychological problems. He had studied at Jesus College Cambridge before serving his articles in his father's office and in 1874, with George Bodley and Thomas Garner, had founded Watts and Company on similar lines to William Morris's interior décor firm, producing furniture, textiles and wallpaper. In 1880, perhaps consciously treading in Pugin's footsteps, he converted to Roman Catholicism much to the horror of his staunchly Anglican family and developed a morbid hatred of Gladstone's Liberalism. By 1884 he was diagnosed as "of unsound mind", eventually being found dead in 1897 at St Pancras Station Hotel, ironically one of his father's commissions.

St John the Baptist, Busbridge.

George produced only one design in West Surrey, the church of St. John the Baptist at Busbridge, (St. Mary Magdalene at Reigate being his other Surrey building). St. John the Baptist, built in 1865 is an unusual design for a variety of reasons, not least that, unlike almost every other church, it is aligned north-south rather than east-west, this alignment being dictated by the long narrow site at the confluence of two roads. The design in Bargate stone with shingled central tower sits comfortably in the landscape and it was perhaps inevitable that it should attract the attention of the locality's most influential artist – Gertrude Jekyll – when she moved to the hamlet in 1877. Over the ensuing years a variety of respected artists were commissioned to produce fittings for the church; William Morris designing an altar frontal in c.1870, Edward Burne-Jones contributing stained glass windows made up by Morris & Co. in 1899 and 1905. The Rood and Chancel screen by J. Starkie Gardner were made to designs by Lutyens in 1897. In the churchyard Lutyens produced a war memorial in 1920 and designed tombs for Gertrude and Herbert Jekyll in 1932 and for their mother in 1895.

Giles, son of George jun. was perhaps as influential in his own age as his grandfather had been in his. Though his output never approached that of his grandfather, his designs were produced in an age that sought different messages from its architecture. He was articled to Temple Lushington Moore who was himself a former pupil of Giles's father. His restrained style was perhaps based on that of his master, whose own work was based on a simplified Gothic.

The breadth of Scott's work is perhaps best symbolized by his designs for two ecclesiastical buildings, the great Anglican cathedral at Liverpool (for which Lutyens's Roman Catholic Cathedral was to be the counterpoint), and his monumental chapel at Charterhouse. The Liverpool Cathedral had been conceived in the first years of the new century and was to exemplify the pre-eminence of Empire and Anglicanism. Scott's design had been chosen in competition in 1903 and would be the largest Gothic church in England, one designed moreover by a Roman Catholic and a young one at that (he was just 22).

Memorial Chapel, Charterhouse, Godalming.

His major work in Surrey, the Memorial Chapel at Charterhouse is in a sense the antithesis of his earlier work at Liverpool. While the great cathedral confirmed the primacy of the Anglican faith, a reassurance that all was well with the world, Charterhouse is of another age, an age grown old before its time, a society mourning the loss of an entire generation on the fields of death. It is believed that of all classes of English society, it was the sons of the public school system that suffered most in the Great War. In 1922, Scott came to Charterhouse to erect a monument to those old boys slaughtered in France. To stand today in his creation with one's back to the west door, flanked by the names of 700 Old Carthusians dead in battle, to realize that every seat in that great chapel represents a name on that memorial, is a sobering experience.

While Liverpool was quietly exuberant, Charterhouse is austere, monumental, silent, a guardian of those names. Rising vertically from the playing fields, sheer and unadorned, Scott's Bargate stone walls are broken only by single, tall, widely spaced lancets that rise right to the roof and terminate in gablets, giving an immensely strong vertical element to the design. Inside, this verticality is retained and enforced by the interior treatment of the window splays that are constrained by flanking piers rising up to the roof to become elegant vaulting ribs supporting the ceiling. The east end is apsidal, lit by trefoil windows with an unusual stained glass design, the whole enclosed by a chancel arch of various orders. The spatial relationships at work in the chapel combine with the restrained austerity of the architecture to produce a truly commendable memorial to the fallen of Charterhouse.

Yet strangely, it was another Scott design that ultimately came to be his most lasting and pervasive – his winning design for the red telephone box – which, until recently could be seen in almost every corner of the land. Scott had produced a series of designs for the GPO for pillar boxes, stamp machines and telephone boxes from 1923, his design for the steel K6 box of 1935 becoming the most commonly produced (though he had produced a similar design in reinforced concrete). His familiar red box is now deemed to

Heywood Court, Charterhouse, Godalming

be uneconomical to maintain and has been more or less replaced by a more modern (but uninspired) design. Fortunately a number survive with the protection of local listing.

When Charterhouse found itself, in the late 1960s, in need of accommodation for pupils and staff to replace the old blocks on Charterhouse Hill, it was to another Scott that it turned, to the practice of Sir Giles Scott, Son and Partner. Responsible for major works such as Blue Circle Industry's headquarters at Aldermaston Court in the 1980s and the controversial Guildhall extension, which eventually incorporated newly discovered Roman remains in the 1990s, the practice, latterly under the control of the son – Richard Scott – produced a design for a series of seven accommodation blocks designed as assemblages of polygonal units each with roofs of different heights. The roof-line of each unit was created by an angular truncation of the elevation, producing a most eye-catching silhouette. The largest block, Heywood Court, incorporates the tallest tower and here the truncation is most notable. For a sixties design, (the blocks were designed and built between 1965 and 1974), these are remarkably fresh, betraying none of the datedness of most sixties architecture.

Each block was built in-situ up to first floor level where a massive reinforced concrete ring beam was constructed. From this the remainder of the elevations were built up using precast units with brick cladding. The unusual chamfering of the blocks' units, producing a lively irregular façade, was intended to take full advantage of the site and to provide as many study bedrooms as possible with a view across the playing fields to Hindhead and beyond. By changing the position of the wings around a central core and mirroring the plans, it was possible for every block to be different one from another. The Scott office was also used to provide the school with a series of new buildings during the seventies and early eighties in a variety of styles, not always as successful as the accommodation blocks but reflections of the age none-the-less. These included schools of technology and music (1978-83) and a dining hall (1973); and the Ben Travers Theatre (1979) in a quasi-industrial light steel cladding to produce a design not really in harmony with the rest of the school.

All in all, a remarkable dynasty, and one quite unparalleled in the history of architecture. These four generations of Scotts have produced a body of work ranging from workman-like to remarkable, from utilitarian to profound.

Sir George Gilbert Scott's Buildings:

Church of St John the Evangelist, Farncombe. 1847-75

Church of St Mary, Shackleford. 1865

Church of Sts Peter & Paul, Godalming. 1877

George Gilbert Scott jun. Buildings:

Church of St John the Baptist, Busbridge. 1865-7

Sir Giles Gilbert Scott's Buildings:

Memorial Chapel, Charterhouse. 1922-7

Richard Gilbert Scott's Buildings:

Seven Accommodation Blocks, Charterhouse. 1965-74

Dining Hall, Charterhouse. 1973

School of Technology, Charterhouse. 1978-80

School of Music, Charterhouse. 1979-83

Ben Travers Theatre, Charterhouse. 1979-83

Richard Norman Shaw

1831 - 1912

Richard Norman Shaw

1831-1912

"The God of Gods was Shaw. If there was a good job going Shaw got it. If he didn't want it anyone might have it."
Harold Falkner 1938

If anyone could take credit for introducing vernacular elements into country house architecture, it would have been Shaw. He it was that demonstrated through his designs that there was a viable and attractive alternative to the classical or Gothic pile and one moreover that used native styles. His close study of English vernacular traditions and their application to his designs brought about a minor revolution in domestic architecture. It came to be called his "Old English" style, and such was Shaw's influence that very soon it had swept England and much of the United States besides.

Shaw had been born in 1831 in Edinburgh and was first articled to the architect William Burn, and then to Anthony Salvin, but later, in 1859, he moved to the office of George Edmund Street, replacing Philip Webb as his principal assistant. While there he travelled the southern counties to study and draw traditional rural building techniques. Here too, he met William Nesfield and together, on completion of their training, they undertook a further tour, this time of Sussex, for yet more study of the traditional architectural forms of the area. This intensive study was later to pay dividends for in 1863, with Nesfield as his partner; Shaw left Street's office to set up in practice and was soon producing vernacular designs for country houses.

But their designs were not mere copies of rural Kentish and Sussex cottages. Their strength came from the way in which vernacular elements – tile hanging, half timbering and rustic stone – were used, often in combination, to produce a more "homely" edifice than the traditionally sombre Palladian or Gothic houses which had up till now been the mainstay of the professional architect. It was this reinterpretation of traditional styles and their application to modern buildings that became known as the "Old English" style and while its use for large buildings attracted much interest, it was its later application to smaller detached and semi-detached houses at Bedford Park that really caught the public imagination and which spawned countless thousands of mock-Tudor suburban semis up and down the country.

The partnership did not only design in "Old English" though, they were equally happy designing in Queen Anne, Gothic or whatever the client wanted. Shaw was not one to let architectural belief get in the way of work. He had no time for those who preached fellowship and a return to a communist work ethic while busily engaging in capitalist venture, inclining to the view that William Morris, for example, far from being a prophet was in fact a money-grubbing hypocrite. So this ease with any style, this lack of architectural principles, was what probably brought the smile to Shaw's face the day a young architect called Edwin Lutyens button-holed him to expound on what he called his "fixed principles." Shaw was experienced enough to know that a long-lasting and busy architectural practice and "fixed principles" were mutually exclusive, a lesson that Lutyens was quick to learn.

Shaw's partnership with Nesfield lasted until 1869. One of Shaw's first designs, Leyswood in Sussex in 1866 was typical of his early "Old English" style; it was built for J.W. Temple, Managing Director of the Shaw, Savill Line, (started by Shaw's brother in the 1850s). In similar vein Upperhouse, Shamley Green in 1874, Pierrepont, Frensham in 1876, and Merrist Wood, Guildford in 1877 were all designed around vernacular themes. Indeed Shaw developed a standardized set of rural elements or treatments which could be applied to any design. Thus the window frame detail for Merrist Wood had already been used for

Pierrepont, Frensham

Pierrepont, while its panelling was the same as that used at Upper House; Pierrepont's bargeboards were to be identical to those used at Wispers etc. While this might again have laid Shaw open to criticism on the grounds of lack of originality, he was merely formalizing a styling convention that most architects kept in their heads or their copy-books.

Shaw's "homeliness" then, proved to be a popular style and showed up-and-coming architects that alternatives to Classical or Gothic designs were to be had if they used their eyes. This lesson was not lost on the assistants that passed through his office in Argyll Street which he still shared with Nesfield even after the end of their partnership. People such as E.J. May, W.R. Letherby, E.S. Prior, Ernest Newton and Gerald Horsley went on to form the backbone of what would become the Arts and Crafts Movement taking Shaw's somewhat stiff style and transforming it into designs altogether more convincing and modest. For if Norman Shaw's designs had one failing, it was their immodest size. The vernacular elements that he had brought to his work had come from rural buildings which were on a much smaller scale than anything Shaw was designing. Consequently, when those elements were applied to houses such as Merrist Wood, with its acres of tile hanging and half-timbering, the essentially homely effect was lost, introducing a discordant note into the composition. It was this lack of conviction in the design that later architects such as Lutyens overcame brilliantly in their designs but with which Shaw often struggled.

Pierrepont at Frensham perfectly illustrates Shaw's tendency to massiveness in his earlier buildings. It is large, very large. A ground floor of light stone gives way to two storeys of close-set half timbered work in stark black and white, a style that, while common in Cheshire, was foreign to Surrey where the timbers and plaster were left unpainted. While the main façade is overpowering, the rear elevation is altogether more pleasing because it is broken into smaller units. Here the timbering is much more successful because there is less of it, a lesson that Shaw later took to heart. This façade too shows Shaw's magnificent chimneys to advantage sailing high above the tiled roof.

Kemnal, Haslemere

Shaw was always an individual and was loathe to bow to convention. At a time when almost all architects felt the need to belong to RIBA and most to SPAB, Shaw preferred membership of the Royal Academy and his acceptance of church restoration commissions effectively debarred him from SPAB. When the discussions and debates among architects about the status of their calling and attempts by RIBA to toughen membership qualification came to a head, it was Shaw who formalized and edited the central arguments in a work entitled, "Architecture – A Profession or an Art."

While Shaw's work on country houses had used vernacular elements including slate tiles, roughcast or rustic stone walls, his town work, while incorporating exposed timber and tile-hanging, tended more towards "Queen Anne." This was especially the case at Bedford Park, a speculative estate development in London and one of the earliest garden suburbs, where the two styles were intermixed in a series of standard house designs suitable for the middle classes.

Another design that tended towards Queen Anne, though with vernacular elements, was Kemnal at Haslemere. Here, the tendency to overpower the observer has been checked in a superb design that is a delight in its understatement. A long thin two-storey house in warm brick with the garden elevation jettied out on white wooden brackets and the entire upper storey authentically tile-hung. The east elevation is stopped by one of Shaw's nicely understated chimneys while the west end is gabled and holds another room at third floor level. Kemnal shows that by 1888, the date of its design, Shaw had perfected the blending of diverse structural elements into a cohesive whole. Here, the observer feels, they are not merely for effect but are an integral part of the building. This is not surprising when one considers a very early Shaw design at Frensham, The Hop House.

Here, a ground floor of sandstone and brick dressings supports a timbered upper storey with tile-hanging above which, while slightly fanciful, is small enough to suggest authenticity. A further wing to the rear again in stone with brick dressings heightens the feel that the observer is

The Hop House, Frensham

viewing an accretive design. It is only the timbering of the first floor that betrays the relative modernity of the design but the result is an extremely picturesque building.

In his later country work, Shaw returned to a vaguely Tudor style such as The Hallams, Shamley Green in 1894. The house is situated among pine trees on Blackheath and is approached along narrow tracks through bracken and rhododendron so that on arrival the visitor is suddenly confronted by the stark half-timbered and tile-hung entrance front, with adjacent two storey bay window, a repeat of that used successfully at Merrist Wood 20 years earlier. The house is composed of two main blocks, the eastern one containing the entrance and grand hall. The two storey entrance porch is typically Tudor in black and white timbered work on a sandstone base and is again reminiscent of the earlier work at Merrist Wood. This leads through into the great hall which is lit by a full height bay window with extravagant leaded glazing. The off-centre entrance and double bay are balanced by a projecting tile-hung block to the left.

Behind the entrance block, the western block is given an altogether lighter treatment. Here, a ground floor of brick with sandstone dressings and a tile-hung upper storey are topped by half-timbered gables at each end of the elevation. The effect is warm and welcoming without the heaviness that is suggested in the entrance front. As always, Shaw's magnificent chimneys soar above the house, massive and dominating; one closes the front elevation while another takes up an entire gable end. These two full height chimneys have been artfully contrived in a mixture of brick and dark local sandstone rubble to suggest a vernacular origin. This was a deceit that Shaw had previously used at Piccards Rough in the library chimney where he instructed the builder, "brick and stone with a few courses of tiles here and there. Please make a very good job of this so that the brickwork may appear to die gradually into the stone work."

While the house is large by today's standards, it is less forbidding than the heavy massing of Merrist Wood and altogether more attractive. Unfortunately for Shaw's buildings, it was this tendency to massiveness that has been

The Hallams, Blackheath

their undoing; several in the area have been demolished because their size and exuberance did not fit the ideals of a later age. In this context, the Capital and Counties Bank in Farnham built in 1890 in timbering with brick infill, a magnificent edifice totally unsuited to its surroundings; and *Alderbrook*, a large tile-hung house of the 1880s in Cranleigh have both been lost though Alderbrook lodge survives, possibly by Shaw. His later town work such as New Scotland Yard 1900-07, could be anything from Queen Anne to Neo-Classical or even Neo-Baroque.

Shaw's lasting testament then was to be a stepping-stone between the Classical and Gothic forms of the early nineteenth century and the free vernacular of the Arts and Crafts Movement that reached its climax in the last decade of the nineteenth century.

Shaw's Buildings:

The Hop House, Kennel Lane, Frensham. 1870

Upperhouse/Stoke Allbrooke/Waverley Cottage/Magnolia Cottage, Upperhouse Lane, Shamley Green. 1874-1887

Pierrepont, Frensham Road, Frensham. 1876

Pierrepont Lodge, Frensham Road, Frensham. 1876

Kemnal Lodge & Kemnal Cottage, Grayswood Road, Haslemere. c.1883

Kemnal, Grayswood Road, Haslemere. 1888

Thirlestane? Haslemere.

The Hallams, Littleford Lane, Blackheath. 1894

Philip Speakman Webb

1831 – 1915

Philip Speakman Webb

1831 – 1915

"Architecture to Webb was first of all a common tradition of honest building."
W.R. Letherby

Letherby had concluded that "Architecture was naturally found out in doing…In a word, architecture is building traditionally", and it was this honesty to traditional building techniques to which Webb had consistently adhered. He was above all an architect's architect: admired, respected, and copied by other architects. Today, his buildings do not excite the unpractised eye but of all the Victorian architects, Webb was their aspiration, even Lutyens uncharacteristically bending the knee to him, "It should be the duty of the present generation to make a faithful and technical record of his work, illustrated by his working drawings, specifications and even quantities, for there was no item in the fabric of his building too small or trivial for him to consider and design to fit its purpose."

Webb was born in Oxford in 1831, the son of a local doctor. On leaving school he was articled to John Billing in Reading before joining the office of George Edmund Street, architect to the Oxford Diocese and becoming his chief assistant. It was here in 1856 that one of those happy meetings of minds occurred when Webb met and became friends with William Morris. That same year Webb moved with Street to London, staying with him until 1859, before leaving to set up practice alone. What turned out to be his first highly influential commission had started as a personal favour to his friend Morris when he was asked to design a house for William and his fiancée Jane Burden in 1858.

His design – The Red House near Bexley Heath in Kent - became a mecca for the Arts and Crafts Movement and exhibited the principles that Webb would subsequently apply to all of his buildings – honesty to local building traditions and materials. The Red House was a simple, almost plain design but exuded the Ruskinian principles of its owner. Not only did Webb design the house, he had to design much of the interior furnishings as well, for Morris to make up. Two years later, Webb joined with Morris in the latter's first foray into interior décor as a business with the founding of Morris, Marshall, Faulkner & Co. This collection of Pre-Raphaelite painters and craftsmen was to have a tremendous influence on house furnishings in the coming years but as a commercial enterprise, struggled in the early years and survived on the commissions obtained from sympathetic patrons and what the partners bought for themselves. Webb produced many of the designs for the company which were then realized not only in paint but in textiles, wood and metal.

The Red House had owed much to Street's designs for similar sized buildings, in particular his vicarages. Its plan and elevations were simple and understated, plain and unpretentious in red brick. But though plain outside, the interior was lavishly decorated by Morris's friends with stained glass and coloured wallpapers and furniture designed by Morris himself. Its design combined the simplicity that Webb had learnt from Street with Webb's dedication to the cause of local traditions in house building; it was quiet, simple, homely.

As Webb's reputation increased his buildings became objects of pilgrimage for younger architectural students eager to learn from him. And since he eschewed publicity and refused to publish his work, this was the only way that many could appreciate his work. His practice relied solely on personal introductions but nonetheless flourished. Although in later years he became the most influential architect of the Arts and Crafts movement, stylistically he could never be defined. Having begun his professional career with fairly strict Gothic principles acquired from his master Street and used to good effect in The Red House, after about 1870, he was happy to incorporate classical elements such as square or segment headed sash windows; so if he felt that a Queen Anne style was required then he would use it, but always bent to his own will, sometimes mixing features from different styles to produce something totally individual. If any stylistic thread ran through his commissions it was the use of local style and material to produce an honest design, devoid of whimsy.

One way in which Webb's influence was able to spread was through his membership of the Society for the Protection of Ancient Buildings. Sir George Gilbert Scott's proposal for the restoration of Tewksbury Cathedral had horrified Morris and was the catalyst for the creation by him of SPAB in 1877. The Society proved popular with the young Arts and Crafts architects who eagerly supported its doctrine that honest repair was preferable to wholesale restoration to a condition that had probably never existed and Webb as a founding member was usually present at its meetings and dinners and open to his fellows.

Webb's old master Street had built a house for himself at Holmbury, near Ewhurst in 1873 and designed (and paid for) its church in 1879 and this was perhaps the reason that Webb obtained a number of commissions in the area. Of his buildings in West Surrey, Joldwynds at Holmbury St.Mary was one of the best known and most frequently visited though this work was lost in a 1930s rebuild by Oliver Hill in a Modern style. Coneyhurst above Ewhurst of 1884-6, Great Tangley Manor of 1886 and Willinghurst of 1887 followed in close succession. While Coneyhurst and Willinghurst were new houses, Great Tangley was an addition to a 15th century house (refronted in the 16th century). Nairn felt Webb's work here to be, "one of the first 19th century additions to an existing house to attempt to reproduce the spirit and deliberately avoid reproducing the letter of the old work." With the building in such safe hands, it is no surprise that the original house and the new addition sit so well together, even such a severe critic as Jekyll giving it the seal of approval.

Webb's design for Mary Ewart's house at Ewhurst -

Coneyhurst on the Hill - of 1884/6 is almost completely lacking in ostentation, so much so that at first one is at a loss to identify its designer at all. But closer inspection begins to bring out the marks of his presence. The internal spaces of the house revolve around the full height hall and its associated staircase which in turn opens out into a mezzanine gallery around three sides of the hall at first floor level. The principle rooms which open off the hall have very wide double doors that can be folded right back to vastly increase the circulation space. The fireplaces are plain and workmanlike much as Webb might have designed and may well be original. Externally all is solid and beautifully finished; the principle elevation has a twin gabled double bay with the weather boarded gables bracketed out at each side. Recessed planes of brickwork on the ground floor provide a blind arcading that enlivens what might have been too quiet a façade.

A side bay in the drawing room supports a small canopied balcony which opens from the main bedroom, the hipped roof of which adds another roof-line to the already busy array of gables while the chimneys are typically large but again fairly plain. Areas of tilehanging are tightly controlled and provide a nice balance to the red brickwork and white woodwork. Unlike some of his contemporaries, Webb was always careful to ensure that his designs included adequate room for the servants and at Coneyhurst, the servant's quarters on the second floor are comfortable and accommodating with good sized rooms.

The abiding theme is lack of ostentation but careful attention to detail to produce a quiet, comfortable home. Only in the central circulating space of the hall has Webb produced something a little more ornate in his careful joinery on the stairs and gallery.

Tangley Manor however was a complete contrast to Coneyhurst. Great Tangley Manor at Wonersh, probably built as an open hall house in the early sixteenth century, has long been noted for its impressive timber framing, its "new" front having been added by John Carril in 1582. At about this time too, the hall was ceiled to produce an upper floor, the

Coneyhurst on the Hill, Ewhurst

ornate king post roof now forming the roof of the main bedroom. Passing through a succession of local families, it was purchased in the mid eighteenth century by Fletcher Norton, later to become Lord Grantley.

In 1885, in the widespread sale of the Grantley family holdings, Great Tangley was purchased by Wickham Flower, a solicitor from London – a fortunate move since Flower was a founding member of the Society for the Protection of Ancient Buildings. Flower brought in his colleague from SPAB – Philip Webb – to oversee the various alterations that Flower felt were needed to bring the house up to his requirements. With the re-excavation of the moat as part of the construction of ornamental gardens around the house, Webb's first job was to design a covered bridge and passage across the moat to a new entrance hall in the former maids' parlour at the west end of the house. This new entrance, aligned with the new bridge across the moat, led into a full-height hall complete with staircase leading to an internal balcony.

Then, in 1893, Webb returned to design for Flower a new extension to the eastern end of the house containing a sitting room on the ground floor with bedrooms over reached by a new staircase. This extension was carefully designed so as not to compete with the existing timber façade of the old house, being finished in coursed sandstone (with galleted joints) and with the first floor elevation in roughcast. The roof ridge was kept at a similar level to the old work and was carried through to twin hipped gables facing the lake to the east. This new sitting room featured a prominently beamed ceiling and full height wainscoting and was fitted out with carpets and furniture from Morris & Co, but was later subject to alterations during conversion to a library that resulted in the redesign of the fireplace and the alteration of the south window. The east window was also altered at this time to produce a single storey bay. The original room layout on the first floor also changed but, the changes aside, the extension remains much as Webb designed it.

The following year, Webb was again approached for a bridge design, this time to span the moat at the east end of the house

Great Tangley Manor, Wonersh

to provide access to the new extension from the lake. This bridge echoes the first bridge somewhat in its timber alignments but had no roof. When examined in 1996, the timbers were found to be extensively decayed and the decision was taken to remove the bridge and replace it with another built to Webb's original drawings.

With Webb's retirement in 1900, Flower's requirement for further alterations to Webb's entrance hall at the west end meant that George Jack, a former assistant, was brought in to oversee the changes. Whether those changes were to Jack's drawings or whether he worked to drawings by Webb is a moot point but a new entrance hall was produced behind Webb's and a new sitting room – to replace that at the east end lost in the conversion to library – was also added by Jack at the western end.

Flower's requirements for Great Tangley provided Webb with a difficult task. He had to find some way of providing for his client's needs while at the same time avoiding any damage to the original house, either from ill-considered internal alteration or from external additions that would detract from the balance and rhythm of the earlier work. That he was able to achieve this – internally by leaving the original core untouched and externally by ensuring that his additions were unobtrusive and unlikely to compete for attention – Webb proved himself a consummate professional.

Today then, while Philip Webb's work may often pass unnoticed, in its day it was hugely influential because, as Margaret Richardson realized, "his buildings provided examples of inventive ways of using traditional building crafts. Webb was solely interested in building craft and hence his buildings do not present a coherent style; none the less his buildings were much visited and admired, in particular his vernacular work in Surrey."

Webb's Buildings:

High Raise, Ewhurst. 1884/6

Coneyhurst on the Hill, Ewhurst. 1885/6

Mendip & Brackenlea, Ewhurst. 1885/6

Great Tangley Manor & Great Tangley Manor West, Wonersh. 1886/94

Willinghurst, Shamley Green. 1887

Coach House, Little Willinghurst, Shamley Green. 1887

Willinghurst Cottage, Shamley Green. 1887

Smithwood Common Lodge? Willinghurst, Shamley Green. 1897

Stroud Lodge? Willinghurst, Shamley Green. 1899

Ralph Nevill

1845 - 1917

Ralph Nevill
1845 - 1917

"There is more real advantage to be gained from a diligent and discriminating study of actual buildings than by the assimilation of any number of text books, valuable as they may be. The more intimately the student is acquainted with old work, the less eager will he be to parade his insufficient powers under the specious but terrible plea of being original."

Ralph Nevill 1889.

William Nevill had a hosiery factory in Catteshall Lane, Godalming from at least 1855 producing "patent fleecy hosiery, Segovia lamb's wool and cotton goods etc" at Langham Mill and his son Ralph had been born in the town on April 23rd 1845. His education was obtained at a private school in Brighton and as a young man he was elected a fellow of the Society of Antiquaries in 1874. That same year, Ralph was advertizing himself as an architect in Kelly's Directory, also based at Langham. Two years later he was articled to Sir George Gilbert Scott and subsequently married Mary Tweed of Honiton in Devon and had one daughter, Beatrice.

His father William may well have been the inspiration for Ralph's membership and interest in the Society of Antiquaries for he had been a founder member of Surrey Archaeological Society in 1864. By the following year Ralph was also a member and both father and son were based in London but by 1880 Ralph was back in Godalming at Langham, appearing two years later again in Kellys as "Nevill Ralph FSA, Architect at 31 High Street Guildford and at Godalming." After 1888 Ralph appears to have worked from the Rolls Chambers, Chancery Lane and later an address at Kensington, London. The family hosiery business appears to have closed around 1890 since it ceases to appear in the local directories. By 1900 he was back in Guildford for good and living firstly at South Hill and the following year at his final address at Clifton House, Castle Hill. It was here that he became ill with pneumonia and died in January 1917, aged 71.

Nevill had an extensive practice in the southern counties but his designs are little known. In West Surrey he designed Snowdenham Hall, Bramley and carried out work on the restoration of St Peter and Paul, Godalming under Scott in 1876-9 and on Pinewood at Wormley around 1870. He was also responsible for additions and alterations to Rake Manor in the 1880s and the extension of Guildford Museum in 1911. He had also been an unsuccessful entrant in the design of Bradford Town Hall in 1869 when he was 24 and successful in the design for All Saints at Paddington in 1895.

Nevill's design for Snowdenham Hall, built in 1886 for Robert Courage grandson of John Courage, the brewer, produced one of the largest country houses in the area. It could almost be one of Shaw's houses; it has that same massiveness coupled with attention to detail that marked out his "Old English" style. Built largely of brick on a Bargate stone base, it is a complex horizontal design of hipped polygonal bays in stone and timber fronting a gabled and tile hung elevation with elegant Shavian chimneys sailing above a single sweeping clay tile roof. The entire western façade is raised up on a Romanesque arched arcade, again in Bargate and brick which also carries a garden terrace.

Nevill did not article to Scott until 1876, and so it must be assumed that he had been able to pick up the fundamentals of the profession from other sources, perhaps even being self taught; this was, after all, in the days prior to RIBA's introduction of examinations. His work on Godalming's church with Scott consisted of alterations intended to increase the capacity of the church to more fully accommodate the town's burgeoning population. This was to be achieved by the removal of the Georgian galleries which would be compensated by enlarged nave aisles and the removal of the old pews in the body of the church, to be

Snowdenham Hall, Bramley

replaced with open benches. The fabric of the church was also to receive a thorough restoration which, after Scott's death, came to include the alteration of the east arch of the tower. This was anathema to Nevill the staunch antiquarian, who was moved to protest to the church authorities that such a move was "contrary to all sound principles of restoration, of which I am a strenuous supporter and which I regard as of great importance, I wish to clearly absolve myself from all connection with this particular matter and to further acquit myself of responsibility by clearly stating my opinion." But by the following year he felt more magnanimous. "I am bound to admit that the church has gained greatly in appearance thereby and that there seems to me no valid archaeological reason against it."

But while Nevill's building designs are a mystery to many, it was for other talents that he became much more widely known. A combination of architectural and archaeological knowledge, although not unusual in a later generation of architects, enabled Nevill to bring to a wider audience the craftsmanship embodied in the vernacular architecture of West Surrey and through a series of articles and more particularly his book "Old Cottage and Domestic Architecture of South West Surrey" of 1889, he was able to demonstrate that the rural building traditions had equal validity as examples of good design. In his introduction he said, "The art of building, to be really living and successful among us, must not depend on the efforts of a few architects, but must be the possession of the whole of those concerned in the building trades. The builder, his clerk and his workmen, may, by diligent study of the good old work that exists all around them, improve themselves just as architects have, since they took to more diligent study...and spare the public the purposeless and wanton atrocities that so disfigure the land." This "good old work" he illustrated with the superb line drawings for which he became so well known in West Surrey and which were aired to an appreciative new audience in the seventies when a local paper ran a series of articles written around them.

Nevill's work had more than a touch of Norman Shaw to it but, especially when adding to an older house, showed a

Rake Manor, Milford

more intimate acquaintance with the vernacular styles of West Surrey. This was particularly so at Rake Manor, Milford where he was asked to make repairs and substantial additions to a fine Elizabethan house. Nevill added a service wing to the main hall, that nicely balanced an original wing at its other end. This older wing he then extended to the rear to form a drawing room. In keeping with Webb's dictum that new work should not copy old, Nevill's work here was obviously different from the original work but such was his understanding of the nature of vernacular that the finished house has a cohesion sadly lacking in some others. It was this service wing that Lutyens subsequently enlarged still further in 1897 and Baillie-Scott in 1910.

Rake was a substantial house built in the early 1600s under the tenure of Henry Bell in Milford, then in the parish of Witley. It had passed through a succession of owners, more concerned, one suspects, with the adjacent mill than the house itself, until bought by Ellis Duncombe Gosling of Busbridge Hall around 1879. Gosling found himself the owner of a property that had seen no substantial modification

for over 250 years and it was to rectify this situation and produce a more commodious abode that Nevill was brought in.

In the several years after 1882 Nevill enlarged the old house by adding a substantial cross-wing to the north end which provided a welcome balance to the existing wing to the south. This new kitchen and servant's wing contained the utilitarian functions previously carried on in the main building. In this way the older part of the house was freed up for use by the family. On the west of the house a single height lean-to was remodelled and within the hall, Nevill created an imposing mantelpiece in the manner of others of 17th century date in the parlour, inscribed with Gosling's initials, while above the new roof soared imposing chimneys reminiscent of Shaw. To the north a new stable block (now Lake Cottage) was constructed and Rake Mill House (now Rake Cottage) remodelled in timber and tile-hanging in a stiff vernacular style.

Lawrence Weaver, writing in 1913, felt that Nevill's work

Rake Court, Milford

here had been carried out, "…when such work was not so well understood as it is today and the building suffered somewhat…" A trifle unfair perhaps for Nevill's work at Rake complimented the old house and allowed it to continue in use when the alternative might so easily have been a thoroughgoing modernization or demolition. Regrettably perhaps for Nevill's legacy, much of his work at Rake was later obscured or swept away by later building work, particularly that by Lutyens in 1899 and Baillie-Scott from 1906, both of whom increased the size of the kitchen wing such that the house was subsequently divided and the former kitchen wing has now become a dwelling in its own right.

In 1911, Surrey Archaeological Society had become painfully aware of the need for new premises and had approached Nevill for a design to be incorporated into the old Society offices in the cottage adjacent to Castle Arch in Quarry Street, Guildford. His design, best described as workmanlike, allowed the Society's expanding collection and its headquarters to be retained in Guildford and also ensured that the old cottage remained in safe hands; not a bad testimony for a self-confessed antiquarian.

Nevill's Buildings:

Pinewood, Brook Road, Wormley. Additions. 1870

Church of St Peter & Paul, Godalming. Alterations. 1877-79

Rake Manor and Court, Milford. Additions. 1882

Snowdenham Hall, Bramley. 1886

Guildford Museum, Quarry Street. 1911

Hugh Thackeray Turner

1850 – 1937

Hugh Thackeray Turner

1850 – 1937

"Here…is shown Turner's intimate knowledge of the building crafts…and his success in making every part of the structure not merely equal to its task, but to look sufficient for its work."
Francis William Troup 1938

Troup was discussing Turner's own house – Westbrook – but could equally have applied the description to any of his work in Surrey. This was Turner's genius; that he understood intimately the traditional building crafts of the locality and could apply them seamlessly to a new building, at once giving the impression of agelessness. His position as secretary of the Society for the Protection of Ancient Buildings, taking over from William Morris shortly after the formation of the society and holding the post for the next 29 years, meant that he was well placed to gain an insight into the old ways. In those early days the SPAB acted as a school of traditional building construction. Turner, although an important exponent of the Arts and Crafts Movement actually produced few buildings in Surrey but their very rarity only adds to their value.

Turner's early life appears to be little known but he was articled to Sir George Gilbert Scott and it was as an apprentice that he took over the secretaryship of SPAB from Morris. After leaving Scott, Turner set up a practice with Eustace Balfour, brother of the future Prime Minister in 1890, working mainly for the Grosvenor Estate in Mayfair designing houses and blocks of flats.

In 1888, Turner married April Powell, daughter of Thomas Wilde Powell of Guildford. Norman Shaw had designed Powell's house – Piccards Rough – ten years before. It was Thomas Wilde Powell that now gave him his first local commission – an experiment in social housing – in 1894 in Guildford. The design, for Wycliffe Buildings in Portsmouth Road, was no easy task. The site was a triangle bounded by three roads but Turner's design used this limitation to produce what Pevsner called, "…quite the best of its kind in the country, beautifully adapted to an awkward, wedge-shaped sloping site, with all the subtle play of gables and eaves which the LCC used a little later." The finished building was administered by Non-Conformist trustees for the use of deserving local citizens, preferably those who practiced abstinence. Turner went on to design two more buildings in Guildford both close to Wycliffe Buildings. Mead Cottage built in 1895, of Bargate stone, as were all his local buildings, and The Court built in 1902, wherein Turner experimented with the use of concrete for the floors of the various storeys, projecting the uppermost floor out to form the generous eaves.

The use of Bargate stone by Turner for his buildings in the area was not novel but had, in fact, a long history. The stone is a hard calcareous sandstone which has been quarried from the hills of Godalming for hundreds of years to provide the principle building material for the area. It was used in the Romano-British farmstead at Binscombe and in the parish church of Godalming and only fell out of use after the Second World War.

In 1899, Turner had decided that his family should live in the Guildford area and obtained a virgin site on a hill overlooking Godalming on which to build a house. The result – Westbrook – is a masterpiece of the architects work, an embodiment of the principles of the Arts and Crafts movement. Built as usual in locally occurring Bargate stone, as are many of the local buildings, Westbrook, set in its garden laid out by Gertrude Jekyll, appears timeless.

Jekyll was not given to over praising the individual, but of Turner she wrote that, "When an architect of ripe experience

Westbrook, Godalming

and keen sensibility plans a house and garden for his own home, one may look for something more than usually interesting and in Westbrook one is not disappointed." Lawrence Weaver, writing in Country Life in 1912 thought that Westbrook was, "...simple, unaffected, owing nothing, or at least singularly little, to the spirit of the Renaissance; it shows what can be done by using local materials in a straightforward yet thoughtful fashion."

But as Gradidge points out, "Unaffected certainly, but unsophisticated it is not." The apparent simplicity hides complexity, the straightforwardness hides artfulness. This is no simple copy of a vernacular building but the product of years of design and structural experimentation. Westbrook is built of Bargate stone and, unusually in West Surrey, even the gables and window mullions are of stone rather than the more traditional oak and tile-hanging. The entrance court is to the north and is dominated by a wide stone gabled porch supported by a massive oak beam resting on twinned stone columns. Although imposing, the roof and local materials lend it a human scale. This court is flanked by a high garden

wall to the right and the servants' wing to the left and in the corner where the wing joins the main block a small rendered gable forms a porch over the back door. This minor addition to the façade acts to break up the monotony of stone and allowed the architect to drop the eaves line as he turned the corner.

The rear elevation is rather different, rather less formal. Here, all the principal reception rooms face south onto the garden. The great clay-tiled roof sweeps down like a typical West Surrey farmhouse to the top of the ground floor windows. Inserted into this roof are the dormers of the first floor and attic rooms between which the massive stone chimneys rise majestically. The roof is stopped at either end of the elevation by stone gables. The left one forming a projecting wing while the right hand one is recessed slightly behind the rear face and crashes through the roof line to turn the corner to the servants' wing. The result of all this is not the chaos one might expect but the tranquil perfection of a master.

The Phillips Memorial – Godalming

Some years later in 1913 Turner and Jekyll were commissioned to produce a memorial to "Jack" Phillips of Farncombe, who had been the wireless operator on the SS Titanic and had stayed at his post as the great ship was lost. The result – The Phillips Memorial – in a peaceful setting by the banks of the Wey, was a cloistered garden with open arcades of timber posts roofed with clay tiles and backed with (unusually for Turner) soft brick walls. The result is reminiscent of a farmyard complex so typical of the rural West Surrey scene. Again Turner's handling of vernacular materials cannot be faulted and are complemented by the subtle planting of Gertrude Jekyll.

Turner's Buildings:

Westbrook, Godalming. 1899-1900

Phillips Memorial Cloister, Godalming. 1913

Charles Harrison
Townsend

1851 - 1928

Charles Harrison Townsend
1851-1928

"Without question the most remarkable example of a reckless repudiation of tradition among English Architects of that time."
Nicholas Pevsner 1960

Though Pevsner was discussing the large public buildings designed by Townsend - mainly in London - when he made this comment, many of his smaller buildings show a similar repudiation of tradition while at the same time managing to remain part of the environment from which they appear to have grown. This was entirely within the principles that Townsend thought should order the architect's actions. "It is for him to throw into the crucible of his own nature all his learning and all his knowledge, there to be fused and made one, and out of that melting pot to draw an ingot that is to be stamped and shaped as his own personality…Yet remember that in doing your best to make your architecture speak Today rather than the Past, you are not to strive, of set purpose, to be what you or others may call *original*." While shying away from overt displays of originality then, the architect should also avoid copying too closely the work of his predecessors. This distaste of *Copyism* led him to devise (tongue-in-cheek one suspects) a formula that suggested 75% original design and 25% traditional design might result in the most pleasing structure for all concerned.

Townsend was born in Birkenhead in Cheshire in 1851 to Jackson Townsend, a struggling solicitor and Pauline, daughter of a violin playing Polish immigrant. One of six sons and one daughter, the family though artistic struggled financially. As he entered manhood, Charles was articled to a Liverpool architect named Walter Scott. In 1880 the entire family moved down to London in search of a better life and here in 1883 Townsend obtained work with Thomas Lewis Banks who kept an architectural practice in Finsbury Circus though most of the commissions were in the north of England and by 1884 Townsend and Banks had become partners.

In 1886 Townsend travelled abroad to see the sights in Venice, Ravenna and Verona. This was not his first taste of the continent though, having travelled to Normandy in 1875. Both trips may have been in part dictated by his enduring fascination with mosaics and from them to an interest in Romanesque and Byzantine architecture. The reflection of this Romanesque style was already to be seen in the work of the American architect H.H. Richardson and Townsend submitted designs to *The Builder* for two houses in this style by his former colleague S.G. Beaumont who had emigrated to America. The Romanesque was to remain a powerful though unexpected motif for Townsend, one that appeared in his designs throughout his professional life. While at first its use seems alien in the English landscape, it has its precursors in the ecclesiastical architecture of the early Norman period, which had seen a revival in the 1840s and indeed Pugin was not averse to its use, for example at Peperharow. But it was Townsend's use of the Romanesque in commissions other than the ecclesiastical that makes its presence so unusual, especially when used in domestic architecture.

1888 was to prove a significant year for Townsend, becoming a fellow of RIBA and gaining entrance to the Art Workers Guild. With the confidence of others in him thus established, he left Banks and set up in practice in Westminster. Although the Fellowship of RIBA would have been most welcome, it was probably the election to the Art Workers Guild that Townsend really valued and which was to play an enduring role in his life. With some early commissions in Devon for cottages, Townsend then won an ecclesiastical commission in 1892 for the rebuilding of the west front of All Saints church in Knightsbridge. For this work he turned (perhaps unsurprisingly), to Verona, reproducing the Romanesque façade of San Zeno Maggiore. That same year another church commission, this time in rural Surrey, allowed Townsend the freedom to design a

Church of St.Martin, Blackheath

Romanesque building from scratch. The finished work – St. Martins in Blackheath – is at first sight incredible. The immediate impression is of a Spanish or South American Church uprooted from its native soil and dropped into this leafy English backwater. The squat stuccoed and buttressed walls, the massive round headed arched doorway and pantiled roof topped with vestigial bell turret, all conspire to mark this out as a building not of this place. And yet it works. After the initial start of horror, it actually works.

Townsend's link to this tiny village was due to the philanthropy of one Sir William Roberts-Austin (who had commissioned St. Martins) and Mr Henry Prescott. It was Prescott who provided his later work, the building of a Congregational Chapel and a Village Hall. At first sight, the chapel (now Chapel End) bears no resemblance to the church and yet there are subtle links. The massy buttressing of the church is hinted at in the slight buttresses that frame the chapel's façade giving its walls the effect of battering, and the frontage is dominated by a great arched window which again looks back to the great arch of the church's west front.

The Village Hall however owes more to Norman Shaw than the Roman Empire, a simple building with timbered façade on a sloping site.

The year 1892 saw Townsend busy drawing up what was to be the first of three prestigious commissions for large buildings in the capital – The Bishopsgate Institute in the City. The Institute was to be another philanthropic work which aimed to provide the lower classes with the opportunity to educate themselves and opened in 1894. The flamboyance of the façade was to become something of a trademark on these buildings, one that was not always treated kindly by the architectural press. Soon after this, in 1896, Townsend began his next London building – The Horniman Museum in Forest Hill. The museum, built to house the collection of F.J. Horniman MP was unusual in its sparse interior, two adjoining halls, end to end, providing large open areas for the flexible display of artefacts, both topped by barrel vaulting and another flamboyant frontage. His third public building in London – The Whitechapel Art Gallery was begun in 1899 and opened in 1901. Yet again,

Chapel End, Blackheath

that repudiation of tradition that stirred Pevsner was there. Townsend's street façade dominates the building with a massive Romanesque entrance arch flanked by towers and topped by a mosaic (which was never executed.) While his buildings displayed an, at times, bewildering range of originality, the Romanesque arch was the one constant.

With the completion of the Whitechapel Art Gallery and election to Master of the Art Workers Guild in 1903, Townsend was firmly established as one of the major free-thinking architects of the period, yet with hindsight this was the acme of his career. No more major commissions came his way and the inventiveness, the sheer originality that had marked his work faded. It is likely that this demise was the result of fickle fashion. After the upsurge of the Gothic Revival and tremendous energy of the Arts and Crafts Movement, fashion had swung back to the once despised style of the neo-Classical Revival. The choice for architects was stark; they now designed in the classical idiom or they ceased to attract commissions. Some like Lutyens made the great leap of faith required to achieve this but others, including many of the Arts and Crafts architects refused to countenance such a betrayal of their beliefs and paid the price with a steady diminution of commissions.

During this time, Townsend returned to Blackheath and busied himself in the village upgrading existing cottages and building others anew. While some were quite modest, others were large by today's standards and while they all stem from the same hand, none appear related to the others. Some, like Combe Green (formally Blatchcombe) betray the architects enthusiasm for the work of Norman Shaw with successive surface treatments in vernacular materials used to break up the strong horizontals, but others such as Cobbins, which Townsend built for himself, appear to offer no antecedents unless it be Voysey's roughcast on the battered walls. Here though are the same buttresses and Romanesque arch that had already made their appearance elsewhere in the village.

With the coming of war in 1914 Townsend's work was

Cobbins, Blackheath

almost done. After a period in the Royal Navy supervising the dazzle painting of warships, there appear to have been no more commissions; his work for the Art Workers Guild keeping him busy. His death in 1928 was marked by a Times Obituary which noted that, "Townsend's death leaves a gap in the dwindling group of men who, in the nineties and later, worked for a revival of interest in architecture and the allied arts on a modern note, respecting tradition but trying to avoid imitation of past styles..." Muthesius was similarly impressed by the original work on his public buildings, believing him to be the architect, "...who has achieved the finest results in the endeavour to find a characteristic style based on a personal vocabulary of forms."

Not a bad epitaph for a man who held firm to his principles and suffered for it and in the process bequeathed the village of Blackheath a significant body of his work.

Townsend's Buildings:

Blatchfield, Blackheath. c.1894

Dickhurst, Haslemere. 1894-5

Church of St. Martin, Blackheath. 1895

Village Hall, Blackheath. 1897

Chapel End, Blackheath. 1901

Combe Green, Blackheath. c.1902/7

Theobalds, Blackheath. c.1902/7

The Vicarage, Blackheath. c.1902/7

Cobbins, Blackheath. c.1902/7

Cheshunt, Blackheath. c.1902/7

Cemetery Chapel, Blackheath. c.1902/7

Rosemary Hill, Blackheath. c.1902/7

Arbuthnot Hall, Shamley Green.1906

Ernest Newton

1856 - 1922

Ernest Newton

1856 - 1922

"The house in which Neo-Georgianism assumed its final impeccable sterility."
Nairn & Pevsner 1962

With a recommendation like that, one would think that Newton had been responsible for some pretty awful designs in his time yet the two considered here represent an attractive and largely successful attempt to incorporate Georgian vernacular elements into more modern designs.

Ernest Newton had been articled to the office of R.N. Shaw in 1873, working as his chief clerk until leaving in 1879 to set up his own practice. With former colleagues from this office, including Letherby, Prior and McCartney, he was a founder member of the Art Workers Guild in 1884, a body dedicated to the encouragement of co-operation between architects, artists and other artist-craftsmen. At first, like so many architects, he worked in the style of his master which in this case, meant Shaw's "Old English" style but out of this grew something rather different. Newton's later work divided into two styles, the one deriving from a Tudor vernacular and the other from neo-Classical or Georgian vernacular. Generally the Georgian style was the more successful, though Nairn and Pevsner were scathing of his work, placing the blame for the return of sterile neo-Classical design in Surrey squarely on his shoulders. "...Red Court at Haslemere of 1894 has all the succeeding decades of sterility implicit in its purse-mouthed exactness." They could only recommend one of his designs – Ardenrun Place in Crowshurst – and that because it had been almost burned to the ground! Whenever a Newton house raised its head, it was knocked back with a scornful comment. Yet he could see that neo-Georgian offered a building style that had naturalized into the English countryside, that offered design elements that would appeal to the country gentry who formed the bulk of his clientele.

At first glance it may seem strange for a founder member of the Art Workers Guild to be working in a neo-Classical style but Newton was no mere copyist. His designs, even when provided with symmetrical facades, retain Arts and Crafts principles such as the thin room and corridor plan. And for Newton it was precisely the plan that mattered; "I emphasize the plan as that is really the house...Building must fall into some sort of style – memory, inherited forms and ideas. But this must be accepted, not sought. Pass all through the mill of your mind and don't use forms unmeaningly, like the buttons on the back of a coat."

His Georgian work, despite Nairn and Pevsner, was perfectly legitimate and in accord with Arts and Crafts tradition. It had, after all, been the core of English design for the best part of two hundred years, and it was this Georgian vernacular (if that is not an oxymoron) that attracted Newton to its possibilities, to the textures and colours that it offered his designs. Muthesius saw those possibilities brought forth in Newton's design for Red Court in Haslemere which he felt, "...illustrates Newton's plain, broad, austere manner and its general appearance is an ideal example of what is called in England today a good house." Newton's success was, he felt, attributable to the "...masterly way in which the qualities of the material are handled and shown to advantage, the excellent work in every material, the subtle juxtaposing of colour in the different materials."

At Red Court in Haslemere, built in 1894 for Louis Wigram, Newton produced what Gavin Stamp called "...a sort of vernacular Georgian with segment headed windows..." If the design is not academic Georgian, Newton's designs seldom were, they were always bent to his own plans. Newton himself said, "the planning is without doubt the most important thing in the designing of a house...A natural

Red Court, Haslemere

architecture is a rational healthy builder's art expressing itself soberly through the medium of masonry and carpentry." The two principle elevations – east and south – are entirely different. The garden elevation is terminated by two full height polygonal parapeted bays between which rise twin gables. The entrance from the garden and the lead covered bay that surmounts it are placed off-centre just enough to break up the symmetry of the frontage. All elevations are in a wonderfully warm red brick which forms a pleasing contrast to the stone dressings and white painted fenestration.

The courtyard façade is altogether more austere but none the less attractive. First glimpsed through the courtyard entrance, this elevation is again centred on a twin gabled theme though here they are separated by a flat roofed entrance tower that rises to the roof. Newton was careful to avoid a rigid symmetry by making the right hand façade a three bay unit, the ground floor including an attractive lead canopied bay window. But on the left unit with only two bays, the missing fenestration looks awkward – there is too much wall. Apart from this minor detail it is a very attractive design.

Feathercombe in Hambledon dates from 1910 and was designed by Newton for Eric Parker as a wedding present from his father-in-law. Parker was editor of *The Field* for many years but is chiefly remembered today for his guide to the Surrey countryside, *The Highways and Byways of Surrey*. He lived at Feathercombe from its first days till his death in 1955 and remarkably, the house has been in the hands of his family since its completion.

The house is laid out as an H with a further wing attached to the entrance façade to form a courtyard. Unlike Red Court, Feathercombe is built of a soft brown brick with dressings in a richer red brick. A full clay tiled roof rises above broad white eaves in a relaxed Queen Anne style. Again, as at Red Court, a broadly symmetrical façade is unbalanced just enough by the irregular placing of the elegant chimneys. The house sits in broad sweeping landscaped gardens laid out by Parker and is once again a very attractive design.

Feathercombe, Hambledon

Newtons Buildings:

Red Court, Scotlands Lane, Haslemere. 1894

Red Court Lodge, Scotlands Lane, Haslemere. 1895

High Wykehurst, Wykehurst Lane, Ewhurst. 1906

Feathercombe, Feathercombe Lane, Hambledon. 1910

Lukyns, Three Mile Road, Ewhurst. 1911

Charles Francis Annesley Voysey

1857 - 1941

Charles Francis Annesley Voysey

1857 - 1941

"We cannot be too simple."
C.F.A. Voysey. 1909

In the 1930s, as the Modern Movement cut a swathe through the picturesque architecture of the previous century, Voysey was horrified to find himself lionized as a pioneer of the movement. He had, after-all, "…railed against the movement's 'vulgarly aggressive' proportions, its 'mountebank eccentricity in detail and windows lying on their sides." Yet the Modern Movement *was* based on the same premise that Voysey applied to his art – a simplifying of form and detail. If the Modernists took it to its logical extremes and produced some of the starkest buildings seen at that time, there was little that Voysey could do about it. By then he was destitute anyway.

Voysey was born a Yorkshireman at Hessle but early on the family had to move south in 1871 after religious scandal engulfed his father, a clergyman. He was later to found the Theistic Church after being expelled from the Church of England for heresy. Their new home in Dulwich, London proved amenable enough and three years later he was articled to J.P. Seddon, an architect in the Puginian tradition engaged on commissions for churches and vicarages. In 1879, Voysey moved to the office of Henry Saxon Snell, at that time busy with designs for new London hospitals and the following year received an invitation to join the office of George Devey. Devey was a master at blending his buildings with the countryside and Voysey would have learnt to use vernacular materials and detail in his designs as well as the strong horizontals of Devey's work.

In many ways Devey was a precursor of the Arts and Crafts Movement and one might have expected Voysey to emerge fully fledged into that tradition. Yet throughout his career, he was his own man. Thus although he admired Pugin and his work was frequently published in the Arts and Crafts press, his designs also made use of machine made items (anathema to all who carried the Arts and Crafts torch). As a member of the Art Worker's Guild he often followed the classic Arts and Crafts plan of long, thin houses with rooms linked by a corridor yet ignored the principle that stressed the use of local materials, preferring his walls finished in rough-cast and his roofs in slate, whatever their locale. Despite his denials, he was recognized early on as an innovative influence of his contemporaries. Lutyens noted the "absence of accepted forms…", while Muthesius thought that, "In both interiors and exteriors he strives for a personal style that shall differ from the styles of the past."

Voysey's style exuded an elegant simplicity and tended to be characterized by pale rough-cast walls with buttressing, extended bands of windows tucked up under projecting eaves, a simple slate roof and solid chimneys. His philosophy was adequately summed up when he stated that, "Simplicity, repose, directness and frankness are moral qualities as essential to good architecture as to good men." A statement that could as easily have come from the Modern Movement. It was this desire to regularize and simplify the architectural form that linked Voysey and the Modernists so effectively and in this sense, Voysey was a harbinger.

In 1882 Voysey left Devey and opened an office in London. As his influence grew, commissions came in from all over the country and in the 1890s he designed a series of houses in West Surrey beginning with Lowicks at Frensham in 1894 for F.J. Horniman, a house that he subsequently added to over the years. Three years later he designed New Place in Haslemere, for A.M. Stedman (better known as the publisher Algernon Methuen). Again he added to this over the years, a lodge, gardener's cottage, stables and summer house in 1899 and new gates and additional gardens in 1901.

Lowicks, Frensham

Lowicks, built as a country retreat for F.J. Horniman MP, in 1894 was a simple and, for that time, a small almost cottagey design that displays several typical Voysey elements such as the battered buttresses and chimneys, the deep eaves gables with brackets this time in wrought iron. The elevations are in roughcast topped with a rustic slate roof through which typically Voysey dormers crowd. As the patron of the Horniman Museum in London (for which Harrison Townsend was commissioned) Horniman normally lived in Forest Hill but Lowicks was retained by the family for many years and Voysey made several alterations to the house in 1898, 1904, 1907 and 1911. This was one of the first houses for which he designed the furniture also and in 1916 produced further alterations, including a new summer house for C. Kerr.

At Shackleford the same year, 1897, he designed an unusual house for the Reverend Leighton Grane at Norney. The entrance elevation of Norney Grange features an unlikely full height porch set off-centre between two projecting gabled wings. The gable of the porch is fully semi-circular and carries a circular window above the front door. This semi-circular treatment of the gable, almost Romanesque in its proportions, is repeated in the entrance hall which features a complex interplay of curves and arches imposed on the strictly rectangular room. The circular window in the gable lights the impressive stairway and first floor landing, the sinuous curves of which are picked up by the close set supports of the banister and mirrored by the arched doorways and semi-circular window of the first floor bathroom which opens into the hall space. The shallow arch of the hall doorways is a device repeated throughout the house though in the most unexpected positions; thus in the principal ground floor room on the entrance frontage the outer wall is carried over the fireplace by such an arch to produce an inglenook. This arch is then mirrored in the marble fire breast by the over mantle which curves out from the body of the breast in just such a curve before dying back into the main structure.

Externally, Voysey used a series of diminishing gables to pick out the varying status of the interior spaces with the

Norney Grange, Shackleford

largest gable over the principal bedroom and the smallest roofing the servant's quarters. Originally at this end of the elevation, Voysey had brought the roof sweeping down to head height but was later commissioned to extend the house with an addition that destroyed this treatment as happened at Greyfriars. His treatment of pebbledash elevations and ashlar dressed fenestration under a slate roof is echoed in the lodge, built prior to the main house. Here too, a first floor bay window echoes the full height bay of the main house.

In 1898, Voysey had produced a very attractive design for a house at Bexhill in Sussex. The house was never executed at Bexhill but two years later, Voysey used it for a commission – Priors Garth - at Hurtmore for F.H. Chambers. The owner however never occupied the house and it was sold in 1901 to Leonard Huxley, a master at nearby Charterhouse. With his wife Julia, Huxley established a girl's school at the house – Prior's Field – which, although strictly for girls, had one male pupil – their son Aldous. When he subsequently came to write the classic *Brave New World*, it was in the countryside of his childhood round Hurtmore that he based its climax, between Puttenham a "…modest little village nine storeys high", and the "… fourteen storey tower of Elstead." In 1904 the school was extended to designs by Thomas Muntzer, one of Voysey's pupils. More recently in 2001, further additions including a new sports hall have been made in a Voyseyian pastiche.

Other major houses that Voysey produced in the area were Greyfriars above Puttenham on the Hogs Back for the Sturgis family in 1896, and Littleholme at Guildown in Guildford in 1907. A number of minor commissions kept him busy in the first decade of the 20th century, often making additions to his earlier houses.

But by now the tide of fickle public taste had shifted again. Arts and Crafts, vernacular and rural architecture were over-shadowed by the surging revival of neo-Classicism with Lutyens riding the wave. Now the choice was clear to all architects who professed allegiance to the art of architecture;

either they shifted with public taste and continued to work or they remained true to their principles and returned to obscurity. Those who felt strongly about their calling were often members of the Art Worker's Guild, and Voysey (elected to the Guild in 1884, its first year), like Harrison Townsend, firmly held that the artistic endeavour of the individual was paramount, that there could be no return to the strict regulation of form that neo-classicism demanded.

So it was that after the Great War, Voysey's work diminished to the point of obscurity and his finances to penury. In an unpublished literary blast in 1923 entitled *Tradition and Individuality in Art,* he had made a belated attack on the regrowth of Classicism but it was a straw in the wind.

Alexander Morton reported in the late 1920s that Voysey had begged him for money or he would, "…have to leave my flat, sell my furniture and bury myself in a slum." Ashbee had run into Voysey in the '30s and had, "…asked him how, as he looked down and out, he was getting on. He, who had built more houses than any of us, shook his head ruefully and said "Any house is good enough to start a car from."

His death in Winchester in 1941 brought to an end the life of an architect for whom integrity came before career, everytime. His houses are individual like their creator. While their roots are to be found in English tradition, they are most definitely not Arts and Crafts and neither are they any other recognizable style; they are simply Voysey, the innovator.

Voysey's Buildings:

Lowicks, Frensham. 1894

Norney Lodge, Shackleford. 1897

Norney Grange, Shackleford. 1897

New Place, Haslemere. 1897

Priorsfield School, Shackleford. 1900

Pair of Cottages, Polecat Lane, Haslemere. 1903

New Place Cottage, Haslemere. 1904

North Cottages, Priorsfield, Shackleford. 1904

The Lodge, Haslemere. 1904

Hambledon Hurst, Hambledon. Major addition. 1919

Francis William Troup

1859 - 1941

Francis William Troup
1859 - 1941

"...a dour uncompromising Scot, who clucks like a hen and roars like a lion yet seldom seems to have anything to say."
C.R. Ashbee

In attempting to draw a vignette of Troup, Ashbee gave perhaps the wrong impression of this very capable Scottish architect, making him sound slightly soft in the head. In fact the animal noises were a party trick that Troup performed for children.

Troup was born at Huntly in Grampian in 1859, the second son of Robert Troup and Margaret MacDonald; Troup's mother had died in 1869 when he was ten. From that date Frank and the other children were brought up by their father and, after attending grammar school in Old Aberdeen, in 1877 he was articled to the Glasgow practice of Campbell Douglas and Sellars. This office had seen a series of noteworthy architects pass through its doors including J.M. Brydon, W. Flockhart and J.M. MacLaren and, in 1860 J.J. Stevenson for whom Troup would later work extensively in London.

By 1883, his initial training complete, Troup moved south to join the office of Stevenson who himself had worked under Sir G.G. Scott. He later recalled that this office was known among the young Scottish architects as the "stepping stone to London", and it was here that Troup stayed (with interruptions) for the next six years. In 1884, in common with some of his contemporaries, Troup enrolled at the Royal Academy Schools under Richard Phené Spiers and it was probably here that he first met Robert Weir Schultz; currently resident in Shaw's office and with whom he would share a life-long friendship.

Troup's first taste of recognition came in 1885 with the award of a Silver Medal by the Royal Academy for a series of measured drawings of the north porch of St Pauls Cathedral, the drawings being printed in *The Builder*. By 1886, Troup had completed his stay both at the Royal Academy and at Stevenson's practice and set out to forge his own career and it was during this period that he appears to have carried out work for J.M. Brydon in London, probably on a scheme for the Edinburgh Municipal Buildings, and the Edinburgh practice of Robert Rowand Anderson where the work was probably on the Imperial Institute designs, work for which Troup was never paid in full, a disagreement arising between himself and Anderson over overtime payments.

In 1887, Troup returned to Stevenson's office as Clerk of Works and, in November 1889 became responsible for the renovation of the fabric of St John's College, Oxford, work that had become rather urgent after thirty feet of the library parapet fell into the quad. In their choice of Stevenson, the college was fortunate for he was a founder member of the Society for the Protection of Ancient Buildings and would ensure that any renovation would be most carefully carried out. With Troup as Clerk of Works, the careful restoration proceeded and it was most likely here that he first became involved with the ornamental leadwork that would later become his trademark.

With Troup's accession to the hallowed halls of RIBA Associateship in 1889, his work with J.J. Stevenson and others appears to have continued though he shared office space with Shultz at Gray's Inn Square. In the summer of 1898 he worked for his fellow Scot Robert Lorimer supervising the construction of Whinfold at Hascombe and Catherine Lodge in Chelsea. At this time too his second cousin Robert Falconer MacDonald was also working in the Stevenson office. MacDonald was responsible for a series of designs in West Surrey in the 1890s for cottages and small

Kingwood Hall, Sandhills

country houses around Haslemere and Hambledon, an area where Troup would soon design his finest house.

Joseph King, staunch Congregationist and son of a Liverpool surgeon was related to Troup through the MacDonald family and in 1894, with his wife Maude, he moved from Hampstead to Grayswood near Haslemere. It was Maude's interest in the crafts that resulted in the creation of a nascent weaving co-operative in the area called the Wheel and Spinner's Guild, which came to be better known as the Haslemere Weaving Industry in 1897. With Maude's sister Ethel and her husband Godfrey Blount, the Kings also founded that same year the Peasant Arts Society which likewise sought to encourage English vernacular craft forms. King soon began to use Troup to produce a series of designs for cottages in the neighbourhood of Witley, the location of which are unknown and, in 1902 he was asked for designs for a house for King and his family, to be called Sandhouse. King's interest in the crafts was equal to Troup's own and from this shared interest emerged a remarkably successful design for a country house.

Sandhouse (now Kingwood Hall and Court) was, and is, a quite remarkable house, for the elevations are built up in polychrome brickwork, the blue headers forming a pronounced diaper pattern which must have been extremely

Kingwood Hall and Court, Sandhills

bright when first built. It had been Ruskin who had advocated the use of what he called "structural polychromy" in building design as a means of adding colour to designs in the manner of the medieval Italian architecture that he so admired. Pugin had also used polychromy and it had been further popularized by Butterfield and Street in the 1850s in their ecclesiological designs. But while Troup was happy to design in the Arts and Crafts or Gothic manner, he did not feel constrained by its guiding principles as some did. At Kingwood Hall & Court , vernacular elements are combined with distinctly classical forms such as the columns supporting the entrance porch (shades of Thackeray Turner's Westbrook) and the (almost) stringent symmetry of the façade.

This alliance of formalism with Arts and Crafts changefulness produced a very attractive house and Troup's attention to detail externally was carried through to his interior work as well. The careful carving of the staircase and the craftsmanship applied to the leadwork on the house, which Troup carried out with his colleague William Dodds,

resulted in one of his most impressive works, yet it appears to be the only large country house that he ever designed. Blount was later to produce a rustic frieze that ran around the walls of the hall above the panelling and that detracted somewhat from the sparse simplicity of this important circulating space but this has long since disappeared.

From about 1905, Troup designed a series of very small cottages that he felt offered an inexpensive means of obtaining a roof over ones head. His first design, for E.P. King, was built in Downton, near Lymington Hanpshire, and made use of the latest materials to produce a five-roomed two-storey cottage at the amazing price of £148. The timber-framed building was set on a concrete raft and faced with rendered steel laths and roofed with tiles. Later that year, Troup entered another design to St. Loe Strachey's Cheap Cottage Exhibition at Letchworth, which, though slightly larger (this design included a walk-in larder and earth closet), was only £2 more expensive and came with weather-boarded walls. His efforts won him first prize and his design was used as the basis for a series of designs by others in an attempt to provide the market with a means of inexpensive housing for the working classes.

Troup's attention to detail and his efforts to ensure that his designs were sound and satisfactory for his clients, made him a sought after architect. By 1914 he was awarded the commission to design a new hall for the Art Workers Guild in Queen Square, London. His design, rather than following Arts and Crafts precepts, was a free interpretation of neo-Classical (or Georgian) elements. It backed onto the original building, a Queen Anne house, which may explain Troup's use of the Georgian medium but his classical niches carrying busts of the heroes of the Arts and Crafts movement must have taken some swallowing by some members. Also in 1914, Troup obtained a commission at Hascombe to design additions to Winkworth Farm, a building that had already seen work by Lutyens in 1895 and Coleridge in 1908.

After the Great War, Troup was able to continue to run a commercial practice (unlike many of his contemporaries) by acting as consulting Architect to the Home Office and the Metropolitan Police, producing designs for a number of asylums; at the Royal Albert Hall also as a consulting architect, and working under Herbert Baker on the extensive rebuilding of the Bank of England. Throughout these years his devotion to the craft cause brought a series of offices and recognition; he was variously Secretary to the Arts and Crafts Exhibition Society and the Art Workers Guild (he had joined in 1895), executive committee member and Hon. Secretary for the Society for the Protection of Ancient Buildings; was elected Master of the Art Workers Guild in 1923 and Fellow of the Society of Antiquaries in 1926.

And though he was first and foremost an Arts and Crafts architect, he never turned his back on the revolution in building materials that was going on all around him. His early cottages had made use of concrete, steel lathing and at Blackfriars House in the City, he made use of a steel framed construction covered with white faience – a glazed ceramic ware.

But it had undoubtedly been Troup's close links with the crafts and craftsmen that caused Letherby, as Director of the newly opened Central School of Arts and Crafts in 1896 to invite Troup to join the staff to teach his favourite subject – Leadwork. Here he worked with William Dodds, a registered plumber, to impart the mysteries of lead and its ornamental crafting to his classes. The almost lost craft of decorative leadwork can be seen on many of Troup's houses and especially on Kingwood Hall and Court, yet today it has become once more an almost lost craft.

Troup then was a far more complex character than Ashbee's unflattering portrait suggests. He enunciated his passionate belief in the value of the building crafts in 1923, "Real architecture in combining and unifying the crafts bestows on each its best opportunity. At its best architecture is the spirit which should permeate this union of the crafts, blending and fusing them into a single whole. Thus architecture is at least the matrix of the crafts." Moreover he was one of the few Arts and Crafts architects able to accommodate himself to the changing requirements of the twentieth century. And if that accommodation meant compromise in design, it at least meant that this craftsman's friend could still play an active part in the new age.

Troup's Buildings:

Kingwood Hall and Court, Sandhills. 1902

Kingwood Coach House, Sandhills. 1902

Kingwood Lodge, Sandhills. 1902

Kingwood Stables, Sandhills. 1902

The County Architects

1860-1991

The County Architects

1860-1991

"While it would be presumptuous to regard the present as the end of an era, it is in many ways a new beginning. A time to celebrate achievement, not in a valedictory sense but to urge the continuing need to encourage imagination, creativity, wit and the pursuit of excellence in architecture for Surrey."

Henry Chetwynd-Stapylton 1991

The disparate political structure of local government prior to the mid 19th century was served by an amalgam of offices, created on a seemingly ad-hoc basis, to administer a variety of requirements – Overseers of the Poor, Highway Surveyors, Boards of Guardians etc, often working in an honorary capacity, whose power to effect change was severely limited. But with the rapid pace of change in the country came a series of thoroughgoing reforms of local government and the growth of specialized departments staffed by full-time officials. This was particularly evident in the field of education; where previously the provision of schools had been left to the church and chapel societies – The British And Foreign Schools Society and The National Society for the Education of the Poor in the Principles of the Established Church – from 1870 the Education Act required that local boards be set up to ensure the adequate provision of educational establishments. Throughout the century local government at County, Town and Parish level became more and more organized.

As far as the provision of community buildings was concerned, this had hitherto been left to local benefactors or charitable bodies to provide, there was no political structure in place to control provision, other than the part-time office of County Surveyor of Bridges and Public Works which was more a fire-fighting role than a provider of new structures. In this position in 1860 for Surrey was Mr Edward Lapidge and in that year he died, to be replaced with Charles Henry Howell, himself a partner in a firm of surveyors. Howell's appointment however was of great interest because for the first time, the post had been filled by a qualified architect, Howell having become an associate of the IBA in 1848.

Despite being a surveyor, Howell was first and foremost an architect, designing a variety of municipal buildings prior to his county appointment including the schools at Farncombe and Guildford, Police Stations at Egham and Bagshot and the church at Shamley Green. With his appointment, although not strictly within his remit, he continued to design a wide range of buildings for the county as it in turn became responsible for more social provision. The county however was reluctant to commit scarce money to the many projects that it was responsible for and often sought to convert an existing building to a new use rather than pay out for the construction of a new building. Whilst this policy appeared to cost less in the short term, Howell pointed out that, "…the practice of making constant additions and alterations must always prove expensive and wasteful and the only person who derives any advantage from it is your architect."

Howell's architecture was modest but perfectly suited to the unpretentious streetscapes and rural settings that they occupied. Usually finished in red brick with clay-tiled roof, many of his commissions are still in every-day use, familiar and well-liked structures enhancing our villages and towns.

By 1888, Howell was due to retire having reached 65. It seemed that this architect's time had come. However, that same year the Local Government Act reached the Statute Book laying the foundations for the creation of modern County Councils, and in Surrey there was urgent need for a more fitting and commodious setting for the county seat. Thus it was that the rules were bent to allow the County Surveyor to remain in office for another five years; time enough, it was hoped, to provide a suitable design for a County Hall to be built at Kingston-upon-Thames. Howell's

Farncombe Day Centre

design for the County Hall was nothing if not lively. A Gothic medley verging on the Baroque, it was hailed in the press as palatial and luxurious and is still fulfilling its original purpose more than one hundred years later.

With the completion of his most ambitious project in 1893, Howell at last retired and handed over the reins to his assistant who also happened to be his son. Frank Howell continued to provide the county with modest buildings in the idiom of his father, such as the Police Station at Cranleigh in 1902 and court buildings at Camberley and Woking. In 1904 Howell junior became the first President of the County Surveyors Society and four years later, having worked for the county for some thirty years, he resigned. Quite what the circumstances were that prompted his departure are

unknown but it marked a watershed in the way in which the posts of Surveyor and Architect had previously been treated at County level.

Henceforth, at least for the next forty years, Surrey's architectural requirements were to be contracted out to private enterprise. The County had quite enough on its plate as it was for the 1902 Education Act had made County Councils responsible for the provision of elementary education. This was added to its continuing battle to provide adequate secondary education and showed up the lamentable lack of facilities to handle such requirements. It was decided to appoint the London firm of Jarvis and Richards to take on the ambitious task of providing sufficient buildings to accommodate the new educational needs. Within four years they had completed 28 new elementary schools with another 11 in build and seven new secondary and technical schools including Farnham Grammar School in 1906. With such a successful record, it was no surprise that Jarvis and Richards were retained until the Second World War to fulfil the county's architectural requirements.

With the continued refining of local government processes, Surrey underwent a series of administrative changes in the late 1920s including those which brought the previously independent Education Department within the mainstream County structure and in 1929 the creation of a County Building Department overseen by a Building Surveyor. The job went to one Edwin Finn, RIBA Associate. While works over £2000 were still contracted out, Finn was on hand to deal with any smaller works and to offer valuable advice to the council concerning architectural matters and this new arrangement soon paid dividends. Throughout the thirties, Finn and his department provided the County with a wide range of smaller buildings but at the beginning of World War Two, Mr Finn enlisted and left to fight for his country and on his eventual return, retired.

Finn's eminent departmental leadership was not wasted however, for in 1945 on the foundations of his efforts arose a brand new edifice – the County Architect's Department – under John Harrison as County Architect. As yet a department in name only, Harrison had the task of assembling a multi-disciplinary team of over one hundred professionals which could grasp the nettle of post war reconstruction and move forward into the architectural utopia that beckoned. With the eventual staffing and operation of the department, Jarvis and Richards were cast adrift though certain contracts were still contracted out.

By 1950 the department had grown to 115 with a budget of £1.75M for building programmes and another £400,000 for maintenance works. During these times of economic constraint the department continued to provide the county and its inhabitants with a professional architectural service and a range of up-to-date buildings, usually in a traditional red brick and pitch roofed style that looked right for Surrey.

But with the transition to the "swinging Sixties" it was inevitable that architecture would be caught up in the changing philosophies that were sweeping through the arts and every other sphere of intellectual activity and this change was presaged in architecture by buildings such as Godalming Library. This transitional design featured the traditional use of brick load bearing walls but combined it with the large expanses of glazing and flat roof (since replaced with a pitched example) which would become so common in later - system built - designs. The emphasis here was on human scale and accessibility, attributes that it displays admirably after 30 years, though the end result lacks the friendliness of more traditional designs.

It was now 1962 and, it seemed, it was the lot of another of the County's eminent architects to add his piece to County Hall before he would be allowed to retire and thus Harrison, already 65 set to designing a west wing in a classical style to further embellish Surrey's citadel. That done, in 1963, Harrison at last could retire, his parting marking a watershed in building design at County level, a division between what might loosely be termed traditional and modern styles.

Harrison had been a tower of strength at County Hall, his replacement would need to be exceptional and in Raymond Ash, Surrey got that and more. His arrival coincided with great changes in the world of architecture. The perceived need to build vast quantities of housing had become the hot political issue of the day and successive governments vied with each other to lay claim to be the party of "the people" by providing them with a roof over their heads. The fact that most already had one was quietly ignored and in the spurious name of "slum clearance", whole communities were swept away and rehoused in tower blocks and massive housing estates. To achieve this level of house building, the traditional brick and tile low-rise building gave way to factory built prefabricated standard units, which could be used in multiples to speed the creation of housing or community buildings. This was "system building" and versions of it would be used for the next two decades in an attempt to provide maximum numbers of buildings at minimum cost and at its best, this was achieved; at its worst

Police Station, Godalming

the country was scarred by the creation of new slums which would be demolished less than three decades after their construction.

Raymond Ash had trained at the Birmingham School of Architecture and after the war, had practised at Coventry in the City Architect's office responsible for the rebuilding of that devastated city. In 1951 he became Deputy City Architect at Newcastle before moving to the same position in Birmingham in 1960. The rapid rebuilding in these cities gave Ash much experience in modern building and design technique and in Surrey he now set to, to use the best aspects of system building to provide the county with its schools and public buildings.

The use of prefabricated concrete sections to create substantial buildings was evident in Ash's provision of new Police Stations at Godalming in 1966 and at Guildford in the mid-seventies. Godalming in particular has been criticized as being ugly and out of context though Nairn and Pevsner were more encouraging, "…a good simple block at the top of the hill…very Corbusian." While strongly reminiscent of Le Corbusier in the structural mass being supported on thin columns, here instead of a stark white concrete box, the principle colouring is derived from the dark, almost purple brickwork contrasting strongly with the white of the concrete skeleton and the serpentine stairways that flank the main elevation. This building is likely to be lost in a forthcoming redevelopment, and while it seemed right at the time, few will mourn its passing though with suitable restoration of the façade, its merits might more easily be seen.

Education was, as always, foremost in the department's workload and an attempt was made to set up a forum with other county authorities to encourage the exchange of ideas and the development of new building techniques in the educational sphere. The result was MACE – the Metropolitan Consortium for Education - which operated more or less successfully until the mid seventies. During this time Ash's department produced designs for schools employing modern techniques and materials at Park Mead in Cranleigh, and at Heath End and Upper Hale between

New Hall, Hale Primary School

1966-8. In these a girder framework was used to support a mix of concrete, brick and glass elevations providing well lit, open structures, if rather utilitarian in appearance. More successful was Ash's 1969 design for the West Surrey College of Art and Design (now SIAD – the Surrey Institute of Art and Design) at Farnham. Here much use was made of rich red brick (in a conscious acknowledgement of Farnham's earlier architecture) to produce a series of low-rise buildings arranged around open planted courtyards. Because the layout is inward looking, the effect, while austere from outside is warm and welcoming within. Expansion has continued here throughout the intervening years with the addition of a studio block and library in 1996 and a student village in 1997 under the watchful eye of Property Services.

The changes in Local Government boundaries in the sixties and seventies inevitably reached even into the Architect's Department, for one side-effect was that Surrey's headquarters at County Hall were no longer situate in the County. Plans were drawn up to build a new headquarters in Guildford and much work completed on the design. But the preferred site at Stoke Park aroused much opposition and subsequent delay, eventually leading to a House of Lords ruling against the project in 1975. But by then, even with assent, it seemed unlikely that construction would have proceeded. National economic reverses were crippling Local Authority budgets, the days of large capital projects were over and the plan was scrapped.

With the loss of many projects in the seventies the department, with a staff of over 400, now entered a period of contraction, the better to reflect the smaller and tighter budgetary programmes that events dictated. As if to add tragedy to indignity no sooner had the department reorganized than in 1978 came the death of Raymond Ash. His loss was keenly felt, another watershed passed, his replacement was his deputy Henry Chetwynd Stapylton.

Chetwynd-Stapylton had come from Hertfordshire where he had served as Assistant County Architect. With early training at Liverpool's School of Architecture, he had joined

Vernon House extension, Farnham

Hertfordshire County Council in 1953, finally leaving to join Surrey in 1973 and was confirmed as the new County Architect in 1979. Within the straitjacket of continuing budgetary restraint, the now leaner department continued the work of promoting designs for the county's many requirements. But it was not all Health Centres and old people's homes. In June 1978 Norman Shaw's remarkable composition at Merrist Wood, now the home of the County's Agricultural College, was largely destroyed by fire. A bold decision was taken to restore (or rather rebuild) the house and working to Shaw's original drawings, this was achieved; a fitting tribute to an outstanding architect.

Chetwynd-Stapylton's retirement in 1986 brought his deputy Ian Bobbett to the fore. Bobbett had come from Dorset where he had been Assistant County Architect. As deputy under Chetwynd-Stapylton, Bobbett had been intimately involved in the continuing provision of school buildings for Surrey and the use of innovative construction techniques to produce flexible open and friendly buildings within the tight budgets available. Binscombe County First School completed in 1983 was one of the first to make use of these new ideas based on a timber-framed structure with an external cladding of brick. But while this process seemed suitable for the tight constraint of public buildings, they were less successful when used by developers to produce houses. Poor quality control on site meant that many houses built using this method in the eighties suffered from rot in the factory produced timber frames.

Other projects commissioned during the eighties revolved around the reorganization of the Library Service and the need to modernize the existing buildings or construct anew. In Cranleigh the library had grown out of the reading room of the village's former Lady Peake Institute. A new site had been acquired in the High Street and a sympathetic design which drew heavily on the wealden vernacular style of the locality, produced in local brick and clay tile. The result was an excellent building which reflects the traditional aspects of the area's architecture in a completely modern way. In Farnham the library was again housed in another building - Vernon House - a much-loved local feature and various plans to replace it or add an extension had been mooted in the seventies. Eventually in 1986 plans were drawn up to build a new library in the garden to the rear, to be linked to the house by a glazed corridor. The single storey extension completed in 1990 again reflected the character of many of Farnham's neo-classical buildings but in an entirely modern way, producing a pavilion that complements rather than dominates the old house.

The school at Upper Hale had, by the 1980s, found itself in dire need of extra class space. The school had been set up in the 1840s under the auspices of Bishop Sumner in attractive buildings faced with the large rounded flints common to the area. A solution to the lack of space was found by providing a new hall behind the old school that would thus free up the earlier hall for other activities. This new hall was designed as a free standing building with brick quoined elevations again faced with whole flints to mirror the original buildings, and with a clay tiled half hipped roof. Opened in 1990, it received a Civic Trust award for a design that was considered "exemplary."

By the late eighties, the ever-present rigours of economic constraint and the need to pare costs to the bone revived a previously floated plan to merge the Architectural Department with those of Valuers and Estates Surveyors. Although it quietly dropped out of view, it was never far away and in 1990, with only two projects of any size on the books, the earlier plan now became reality. The new department now became Property Services under Bobbett as Director, its new role being an enabling one with most of its staff and all of its projects contracted out to W.S. Atkins.

While the architectural work of the County and its architects appeared to be at an end, in reality it was just another step in the continuing evolution of architectural services in Surrey. The contribution of the County Architect's Department and its predecessors to the stock of buildings in the county has been tremendous, producing much to be proud of and enhancing Surrey's street scene. The successors to the old department – Property Services and now Construction Management – continue to care for those buildings and to provide a link with the people who produced them.

Buildings produced by or for county architects and the County Architect's Department:

Farncombe School, (now Day Centre) Godalming. Charles Henry Howell. 1857

Christchurch, Shamley Green. Charles Henry Howell. 1863

Police Station, Horsham Road, Cranleigh. Frank Howell. 1902

Grammar School, Farnham. Jarvis & Richards. 1906

Library, Bridge Street, Godalming. John Harrison. 1955-60?

Glebelands County Secondary School, Parsonage Road, Cranleigh. John Harrison? 1958

Police Station, Longbridge, Farnham. John Harrison. 1950s

Park Mead First and Middle Schools, Cranleigh. Raymond Ash. 1966-8

Police Station, Godalming. Raymond Ash. 1966-8

Old Peoples Homes, Farnham. Raymond Ash. 1967-9

Health Centre, Farnham. Raymond Ash. 1967-8

Upper Hale Primary School. Raymond Ash. 1967-8

Heath End Secondary School. Raymond Ash. 1966-8

Surrey Institute of Art and Design, Falkner Road, Farnham. Raymond Ash. 1969

Binscombe County First School, Godalming. Henry Chetwynd-Stapylton. 1982-3

Library, High Street, Cranleigh. Henry Chetwynd-Stapylton. 1985

Library, Vernon House, Farnham. Ian Bobbett. 1990

Hall, Hale County Middle School. Ian Bobbett. 1990

SIAD Studio & Library, Farnham. Nick Evans for Property Services Department 1996

SIAD Student Village, Farnham. Nick Evans for Property Services Department 1997

Edwin Landseer Lutyens

1869 - 1944

Edwin Landseer Lutyens
1869 - 1944

"Sir Edwin Lutyens plays as it were, the part of saint in English Architecture and he is the perfect candidate for the role, too humorous, too aloof for adulation to spoil or influence him or his work."

Clough Williams-Ellis 1925

It is perhaps to be expected that the foremost architect of the nineteenth and twentieth centuries should have had an artistic parentage. Charles Lutyens had obtained a commission in the army in 1848 and immediately moved to Montreal where he met his wife Mary. But Charles was a skilled draughtsman and painter as well as an accomplished sculptor and in 1857 he retired from the army to pursue an artistic career as a painter of horses. That he was able to take this step was largely due to his friendship with Sir Edwin Landseer, himself a highly popular artist. Through Landseer, Charles met people of influence and was able to make a success of his endeavour and enjoy a comfortable income that enabled him to purchase a house in Thursley as well as his London house.

It was here at Onslow Square in 1869 that Edwin was born, the tenth child of this large family with Sir Edwin Landseer as godfather. In 1877, with the addition of the Thursley house to the family's property, a new world opened for the boy. Unable to attend public school due to weakness induced by rheumatic fever, Edwin spent much of his childhood roaming the byways of West Surrey with only himself for company. In later years he told Osbert Sitwell that any talent he had, "…was due to a long illness as a boy, which afforded me time to think, and subsequent ill-health, because I was not allowed to play games, and so had to teach myself, for my enjoyment, to use my eyes instead of my feet." Edwin developed into a shy but able child who hid his nervousness behind a jokey persona and a fondness for puns. He felt at times that the absence of a proper education had hindered his ability to mix with the rich and successful who were his clients and, in later life, fellow committee members and therefore made extra effort to amuse them. It seemed that he

was successful in this for he was considered a popular guest at social gatherings in London.

He developed a fascination for houses and their construction, spending many hours sketching them on glass and haunted the carpenter's shop at Thursley and Tickner's builder's yard at Godalming. From an early age then, Lutyens's future was being literally sketched out and by his teenage years it was obvious that architecture would be an admirably suitable occupation for the boy. Consequently in 1885 "Ned" was enrolled at the Kensington School of Art to study architecture but left before the completion of the course having, in his opinion, learned all there was to learn on the subject.

Two years later Lutyens was articled to the office of Ernest George and here met Herbert Baker the chief assistant, with whom he would collaborate many years later on the designs for New Delhi. It had not been his first choice; he had wanted to work with Norman Shaw but so too did half the architectural students of the country. Baker described many years later the arrival of this precocious young man in their midst. Lutyens, he said, "though joking through his short pupilage, quickly absorbed all that was best worth learning: he puzzled us at first, but we soon found that he seemed to know by intuition some great truths of our art which were not to be learnt there." His pretence of never sketching but of retaining all in memory must have proved irritating to his fellow pupils in the office but his consummate ability showed an exceptional talent already at work.

Undoubtedly, Lutyens's pupilage in the busy George office refined and developed his as yet uneven abilities and taught the nuts and bolts of an architect's business. While still there he had been assiduous in entering designs for numerous competitions and had been surprisingly successful. His first commission now arrived in his home village of Thursley. This was for the alteration of a pair of cottages for E. Gray into a single dwelling –The Corner – in 1888. His early work drew heavily on the techniques and materials with which he had become so familiar in West Surrey and which were now entering into vogue through the work of Shaw, Devey and others. His first large commission, at Crooksbury in 1889 for a family friend, drew extensively on Shaw's "Old English" style with timbering and tile hanging much in evidence and much later he returned to add wings in a variety of styles from Tudor to Georgian. This commission almost reduced him to a nervous wreck, he didn't dare go near it until the workmen had retired for the day but it did give him the confidence to set up an office at Gray's Inn Square in London and brought in its wake sufficient work to keep the young architect busy for the next few years.

There now came about one of the pivotal meetings of Lutyens's life, one that shaped his work for the next decade. Gertrude Jekyll had, against all the odds, carved out for herself a respected position in the world of art. Her parents had moved to Bramley from London when she was four. The child of artistic parents and of the well-ordered surroundings of Bramley Park, Jekyll soon developed an independent spirit and an earnest desire to become a painter. Sheer hard work and an innate ability soon earned her the respect of her contemporaries and by 1865 she was exhibiting at the Royal Academy. A meeting with William Morris in 1869 was the catalyst to a broadening of that talent into the complete Arts and Crafts pantheon and a mastering of embroidery, metal work, woodwork and interior decoration. By 1870 she was at the height of her creative powers and had earned her reputation as an artist of repute when the first signs of impending myopia made themselves felt. Her practical character and the inevitability of her condition caused her to shift her artistic needs from the small scale of her embroidery and pictures to what, until now, had been a budding interest – garden design. Here she could still achieve the interplay of colour and form that drove her on, but on a large scale.

With her new house at Munstead ready for her in 1878 she set to on the design and planting of its garden. By 1883 Jekyll was as respected for her gardening abilities as she had been for her earlier artistic endeavours and in that year she had acquired a plot of woodland at Munstead and had spent some years transforming it into her perfect garden. The time had come for a house to be built in this new garden and it was with the young Lutyens as a potential architect that Jekyll was concerned. It was these two personalities then, both deeply imbued with the rural spirit of West Surrey, who met in the garden of Harry Mangles Littleworth Cross at Seale one afternoon in 1889. His first of many subsequent visits to her garden at Munstead stole Lutyens's heart and enchanted him with the possibilities of a perfect fusion of house with nature.

The partnership of the two artists became an enduring friendship with commissions for the one almost always leading to work for the other, for the melding of house with nature, nature with house, was their goal. The materials of the house would be extended into the garden to form the walls, terraces and pergolas; the garden would encroach on the house with climbing plants on the walls and around the door. The gardener's knowledge of local vernacular designs and the architect's understanding of structural form merged to produce a powerful synthesis of man and nature. This partnership was to last for many years, over one hundred garden and house combinations but after 1910, as Lutyens moved away from vernacular designs, they became few. Over the years Lutyens was to design a number of buildings at Munstead and in the surrounding locality, many of them for Jekyll and consequently the area has become a treasure house of his work.

Lutyens's first house for Jekyll was Munstead Wood Hut, a recreation of a West Surrey vernacular cottage and here she lived while work proceeded on her ultimate house – Munstead Wood. Here Lutyens created a work of art for his most discerning client; Jekyll keeping the architect on a close lead so that the finished house was as much her creation as his. Built again with Bargate stone elevations and mellow tiled roof, the result is utterly in accord with its landscape, a

Munstead Wood, Munstead

quiet design with just a hint of timbering in the rear court-yard. The garden elevation is dominated by twin gables flanked by massive brick chimneys, all backed by a great low sweeping roof that holds the design together. The entrance front is subtly detailed with bands of red tile alternating with the Bargate stone in the entrance arch while the slight arch of the window heads is again filled with red banded tiles.

Lutyens was equally careful with the interior design, producing a series of rooms in accord with his client's wishes that draw on vernacular antecedents for their inspiration, though the dining room alone of all the rooms is a strictly classical composition. Unlike most of his other commissions, Munstead Wood was a house built in a pre-existing garden but then, Gertrude Jekyll was a very unusual woman. Her satisfaction with Lutyens's work was evident in her writing, "...from the way it is built it does not stare with newness; it is not new in any way that is disquieting to the eye; it is neither raw nor callow. On the contrary, it almost gives the impression of a comfortable maturity of something like a couple of hundred years. And yet there is nothing sham-old about it; it is not trumped up with any specious or fashionable devices of spurious antiquity; there is no pretending to be anything that it is not – no affectation whatever. But it is designed and built in the thorough and honest spirit of the good work of old days."

The 1890s were for Lutyens a time of experimentation and trial with the vernacular forms that he had absorbed in his early years. Many of his designs from this time are to be found in West Surrey and they show the architect's growing confidence with form and material. The earlier use of strictly observed detail gives way to a more fanciful or whimsical design; certain elements are exaggerated or combined in a way that was never to be found in vernacular work so that while, at first sight, his designs appear perfectly in accord with surrounding styles, on closer inspection it is evident that they are subtly different, that while their roots are in the local soil, the designs have a life of their own.

Red House, Godalming

Houses from this period include the group at Munstead, Fulbrook and Tigbourne Court. It is also in these houses that Lutyens's movement towards Classical design first makes itself dimly felt. While as yet it is confined to the interiors, there is a sense of tension building in the architect as the limitations of vernacular design, though still some way off, are approached and comprehended. But it was also these designs which made Lutyens's name and showed the world just what could be achieved under the banner of the Arts and Crafts Movement.

From 1897, the culmination of Lutyens's genius in handling the disparate elements of composition and vernacular design was reached. Beginning with Orchards at Munstead, his houses and gardens reached their full flowering of perfection. This was followed by Deanery Garden at Sonning in Berkshire, Marshcourt in Hampshire and Little Thakeham in Sussex and others.

But even as he was reaching the climax of this vernacular tradition, Lutyens was experimenting with other forms, and not just Classicism. The same year (1897) that saw work start on Orchards, a difficult site on a steep hill above Godalming inspired Lutyens to produce a design that at first defies definition – The Red House. The entrance front suggests that the house is a typical product of the neo-Georgian pattern book, its conventionally symmetrical façade only jarred by the massy oversized chimneys that frame the elevation. But moving round to the side, it is immediately apparent that the first impression was wrong, for here is an almost Italianate polygonal balcony and porch again framed by massy chimneys. And what may be termed the garden elevation is something different again. Here, the Italianate vision gives way, catching the viewer unawares as a three storey Tudor design complete with castellated parapet looms above. Full height bays with leaded lights on three levels gaze out over the incredibly steep garden and yet more windows inserted seemingly at random impart a strange restlessness to the house and not until the viewer is inside does this unnerving fenestration explain itself.

Pevsner was not sure what to make of it all either. He

decided that it was "..simplified Tudor...an irregular keep-like mass...", the recessional planes of brickwork along the parapet and the great corner chimneys, like towers, adding to this castle-like feel. It is actually a very skilful blending of at least three different styles built around a massive staircase which completely fills the space normally accorded to a hall. From the main entrance, the square staircase both rises up to a top lit landing and plunges down, for the steep sloping site means that the doorway is actually on the first floor. And it is this staircase that is the key to the confusing fenestration for as it winds its way up through the house with innumerable landings, almost every room opens directly off of it, there are no corridors. It is believed that the house was designed for an invalid (it was designed for Rev W.H. Evans, a Charterhouse master) and it may be that this gave Lutyens the opportunity to play.

What does seem likely is that the house was designed to a strict budget. It lacks those little touches that can prove so expensive. The brickwork for the chimneys appears to be stock bricks rather than the smaller ones, specially made that Lutyens favoured for chimneys. The arches appear to again be stock bricks rather than rubbed. And this should not perhaps surprise us since the client was, after all, but a schoolmaster.

By 1906, the earlier tension was breaking through and Classical designs thrust to the fore. Early experiments with the classical medium, such as the Liberal Club at Farnham of 1895 and the classical wing at Crooksbury were built on to produce Heathcote in Yorkshire – a masterly design where composition triumphed. In a letter to Herbert Baker in 1903 Lutyens had spelt out his enthusiasm for the Classical form…"In architecture Palladio is the game!! It is so big – few appreciate it now, and it requires training to value and realize it…To the average man it is dry bones, but under the hand of a Wren it glows and the stiff materials become as plastic clay." Lutyens was that Wren.

The central problem with vernacular styles was that they lacked the authority of the Classical idiom. While perfectly suited to rural locations they failed when applied to municipal buildings in urban environments. Even Gothic appeared uneasy in metropolitan situations. The Classical tradition was being re-examined all over Europe and the new possibilities that it offered Lutyens were eagerly grasped. Shortly he would be given perhaps one of the last great canvases upon which to achieve his vision of perfection, that vision would not be vernacular or Gothic but a transcendent Classical masterpiece.

As noted above, one of his first forays into the classical idiom had been the Liberal Club in Farnham but this highly unusual building is not what it claims. It wants to be a Georgian Gentleman's club but it just doesn't have the money. Built for the local Liberal Party in 1895 and still in its ownership today, money was collected by subscription for a local headquarters and Lutyens approached for a design. Everything about the building shouts economy and one must assume that Lutyens was forced to work on a very tight budget. Within these constraints he was able to provide a typically Classical façade in thin red brick with alternating angular and segmental pediments over the upper windows, much as Inigo Jones had produced on his Banqueting House of 1620. A typical string course delineates the floors and a prominent cornice serves as a parapet. The centrally placed door case with columns and pediment is flanked by symmetrical casements with sills of rubbed brick. All in all, a classic Georgian elevation with just a hint of Queen Anne. However, the red brick façade has no sooner turned the corner onto the side elevations than the rich red bricks are replaced with poor quality local stock brick of a completely different colour. From the rear it can be seen that the usual shallow pitched roof, once of pantiles but now slated, continues down to ground floor level as a cat-slide. Inside, everything is plain, completely devoid of decoration, though the very high ceiling on the first floor - most of which was given over to a single meeting room - lends a certain dignity to the internal space. Altogether a highly unusual design.

In 1911 the King-Emperor George V had announced the intention to move the seat of Government in India from Calcutta to Delhi. Lutyens had been nominated for the

The Liberal Club, Farnham

design of the new Imperial Capital that same year but it was not until the following year that his success was confirmed. However he was not to be given carte blanche; he had to contend with the ideas of other members of the Delhi Planning Committee and, from 1913, his old acquaintance Herbert Baker. In the event it was decided that while Baker would design the Secretariats and the Council House, Lutyens would be responsible for the jewel in the crown – the Viceroy's House. Problems arose over the architectural style of the new capital; should it be European, Indian, Indo-European or, as Lutyens wanted, Renaissance Classicism in the image of Wren. The arguments raged for some time and eventually a fusion of an austere Classical scheme with Oriental additions was adopted with somewhat more success by Lutyens than by Baker. Lutyens felt that Baker's influence on the overall design of the centre had marred the perfection that could have been. Their many disagreements ended with Lutyens conceding defeat – what he called his "Bakerloo."

In their search for a synthesis of eastern and western styles

for New Delhi, Lutyens and Baker ultimately succeeded. The result was sublime and marked the high point of the Classical tradition. In 1931 the year of its official inauguration, Robert Byron wrote, "The traveller looses a breathe, and with it his apprehension and preconceptions. Here is something not merely worthy, but whose like has never been", yet within 16 years the heart of the Empire in India had been given up.

While Lutyens had been creating the "Delhi Order" in India of course, a war had engulfed Europe. At its close the country turned to the architect of Delhi, now knighted, to concretize its loss. The abstract monumentalism, the pure essence of the Classical Tradition that Lutyens had striven for at New Delhi obtained full expression in the series of War Memorials that he was now commissioned to produce. This might have posed problems for there was no precedent for such architecture in Britain. But in South Africa, in the wake of the Boer War, memorials to the dead had been produced both by Lutyens and Baker. In 1917 Lutyens had been approached by the newly formed War Graves Commission to discuss suitable architecture for the cemeteries and it was therefore unsurprising that Lloyd George asked Lutyens to design a "catafalque" for Whitehall in 1919. Lutyens's reply, remembering the great seat in Jekyll's garden at Munstead "…not a catafalque but a cenotaph", led to the unveiling of a permanent memorial to the dead in 1920, a triumph of the sublime that brought him fame as Britain's foremost architect. For the next decade, both war and personal memorials formed a substantial proportion of Lutyens's work at home and abroad.

Throughout the twenties and thirties, Lutyens, (now a RIBA Gold Medal holder), as well as his war memorial work, continued to travel back and forth to New Delhi as new buildings were required. And between these commissions were somehow fitted many others for private residences and commercial premises. Forever haunted by the collapse of his fathers business and subsequent financial ruin, he continued to maintain a busy schedule producing works such as Gledstone Hall in Yorkshire between 1922-26. In its subtle classicism lay all the genius that Lutyens possessed and it was in the classical tradition that Lutyens felt most able to aspire to perfection, to a synthesis of form and material and geometry.

In England, this synthesis should have reached its zenith (if indeed such a thing is possible) in his plans for a Roman Catholic Cathedral in Liverpool. There was a certain irony in this being designed by the nominally Anglican Lutyens since the recent Anglican Cathedral was the design of Sir Giles Gilbert Scott – a Roman Catholic. Lutyens had obtained this commission from Richard Downey the Archbishop of Liverpool in 1929. The design was monumental, twice the size of St. Paul's with a dome larger than St Peter's in Rome and featured the interpenetrating arches springing from different heights that Lutyens had used to great effect on several of his War Memorials and that was based on the Triumphal Arch of Classical Antiquity. Work began in 1933 and had progressed smoothly enough when war intervened and work stopped. Though work recommenced in the mid 1950s, it was evident that the financial situation would debar completion to the original design. In the event the crypt was completed and in 1959 a competition produced a winning design by Sir Frederick Gibberd, which was completed in 1967 on the basal plinth formed by Lutyens's earlier work.

Lutyens did not live to see the abandonment of his work at Liverpool. Its completion would have been a fitting memorial to architecture's Laureate. In his ability to mirror the national mood in the subtle interplay of architectural form and at the same time to define that mood, Lutyens was peerless. With a funeral at Westminster Abbey and interment in the crypt of St Paul's, the synthesis of Lutyens and Wren was finally complete.

Lutyens's Buildings:

The Corner, Thursley Road, Thursley. 1888
Sussex Lodges, Park Hatch, Hascombe. 1890
Hoe Farm House, Hoe Lane, Hascombe. Additions.1890
Crooksbury House, Crooksbury Road, Tilford. 1890
Clock House & Crooksbury House Cottage, Crooksbury Road, Tilford. 1890
Crooksbury House Lodge, Crooksbury Road, Tilford. 1890
Sheephatch House, Tilford. Additions. 1890
Munstead Place, Heath Lane, Busbridge. 1891

continued:

The Quadrangle, Heath Lane, Godalming. 1891
The Conference Store (Former Dairy), Charterhouse School. 1893
Tilford Institute, Tilford Road, Tilford. 1893
Chinthurst Hill, Wonersh. 1893
Close House & Gate House, Chinthurst Hill, Wonersh. 1893
Munstead Wood Hut, Brighton Road, Godalming. 1894
The Hollies & Fir Tree Cottage, North Munstead Lane, Busbridge.1895
The Liberal Club, South Street, Farnham. 1895
The Thunder House, Heath Lane, Godalming. 1895
Winkworth Farm, Heath Road, Hascombe. Alterations. 1895
Munstead Wood, Heath Lane, Busbridge. 1896
Warrenmere, Portsmouth Road, Thursley. 1896
High Hascombe, Hascombe Court Road, Busbridge. 1896
Little Munstead, North Munstead Lane, Busbridge. 1896
Fulbrook House, Fulbrook Lane, Elstead. 1896
Orchards, Munstead Heath Road, Bramley. 1897
Lodge & Store, Fulbrook Lane, Elstead. 1897
Red House, Frith Hill Road, Godalming. 1897
Boathouse on Thursley Lake, Witley Park, Thursley. 1897
Wood End, Petworth Road, Wormley. 1897
Rake Manor/Court, Milford. Additions. 1897
Bathing Pavilion, Stable Lake, Witley Park, Witley. 1897
Munstead Orchard, Brighton Road, Godalming. 1898
9, 11 & 15 Afton Cottages, Church Road, Milford. 1898
Tigbourne Cottage, Lane End, Hambledon. 1899
Little Leat, Lane End, Hambledon. 1899
Tigbourne Court, Petworth Road, Wormley. 1899
Munstead House, Munstead Heath Road, Busbridge. Additions. 1900
Prospect Cottage, The Street, Thursley. 1900
Cottages, Thursley. 1901
Great Holt, Frensham. 1902
Amesbury School, Hazel Grove, Hindhead. 1903
Millmead House & Garden House, Snowdenham Lane, Bramley. 1904
Barn, stable and shelter shed, High Pitfold, Hindhead. Early 20th century.
Moorhouse, Haslemere.

Harold Falkner

1875 - 1963

Harold Falkner
1875 - 1963

"It can almost be said...that he found Farnham Victorian, and left it all Georgian."
Roderick Gradidge, 1991.

Gradidge was making the point that almost all Falkner's work is concentrated in one town – Farnham, and though he has been closely linked with Lutyens, who was considered the doyen of the Arts and Crafts Movement in his earlier days, his Farnham style was distinctly Georgian in character; often restoring Victorian work to something considered more suited to its Georgian neighbours. But even this is an over-simplification for, in truth, while Falkner's style remained little changed in Farnham itself, after the First World War he began a series of eccentric restorations and new-builds incorporating old farm buildings at Dippenhall which ran in tandem with his other work. It was as if the straight-jacket of neo-Classical design that he forced himself to work within in the town was compensated by this wild disregard for convention in the country.

Although the Falkner family were landowners in Dippenhall, near Farnham, Harold Falkner was born in Bramley at The White House in 1875. The family had moved there shortly after the death of his father but in 1883, the family left Bramley, moving to 24 West Street, Farnham. One of three children, Falkner, with his brother and sister attended a local school but shortly Harold moved to Churcher's College in Petersfield before returning to Farnham and attending the Grammar School next door in West Street. It was here that a lifelong interest in art first flowered and was encouraged by his teacher William H. Allen to such a degree that on leaving Grammar School, Falkner had decided that architecture was the path to follow.

In 1891, he entered the Art School at Farnham to further his studies in art and woodcarving before taking up a two year apprenticeship with a local builder. It was while working with this builder - Frank Birch - that Falkner would have been introduced to the designs of some of the country's leading architects, for Birch had built a number of houses for Norman Shaw, one for Voysey and another next door to Lutyens's Crooksbury. While still serving as an apprentice, Falkner became articled to Reginald Blomfield, moving to his London office in 1894 and while there became a member of the junior section of The Art Workers Guild. His time with Blomfield does not appear to have been too onerous, Falkner's explanation for this being that, "My idea of inking in a drawing and Sir Reginald's did not coincide, so I wasn't overworked."

In 1896, at the age of 21, Falkner inherited a considerable amount of money from his father's estate which allowed him the following year to return to Farnham and set up a practice at his old house. He was now suitably qualified, adequately financed and perfectly placed to start making his mark on his home town and that same year began work on the first of over one hundred designs for Farnham.

With plans to build a new swimming baths in the town to celebrate Victoria's Diamond Jubilee, Falkner not only acted as unpaid architect but contributed to the costs of construction as well. His design of 1897, fronted by a substantial round-arched entrance in warm brick using very narrow rubbed bricks for rustications and voussoirs has stood the test of time and still serves the town, though now as the entrance to the Victoria Garden.

It was about this time that Falkner became acquainted with Gertrude Jekyll, (it has been suggested that he was her Godson), becoming a regular visitor to her house and garden at Munstead and developed an abiding interest in garden design, seeing it – as did Lutyens – as an extension of

Mavins Court, Farnham

architectural design. Also at this time, around 1900, the architect David Niven moved to Farnham from London and Falkner joined the practice of Niven and Wigglesworth as a junior partner while also continuing his own work. Unfortunately, although Falkner designed many houses during this period, the arrangement did not prosper, a number of professional disagreements presaged a final split from the practice after three years. But during his time with his partners Falkner worked on a number of buildings in Farnham including the house for his old art teacher W.H. Allen who of course had encouraged Falkner in his artistic endeavours as a young man. The house, Strangers Corner, was published in the architectural journals of the day and was used as a subject for one of Allen's paintings.

Another house from this period was Mavins Court. Designed around 1906 and exhibited at the Royal Academy the following year as a speculative design. A typically long thin Arts and Crafts plan of south facing principle rooms opening from a corridor running the length of the building, the house is a superb example of just why Falkner was constantly in demand. The front and rear elevations, in warm red brick with darker headers disposed throughout, are both grouped around a triple gabled façade which is cunningly off-centre and balanced by a low sweeping roof with dormers. The porch, which nicely balances the front bay window, is very Classical with vestigial columns and leaded roof. Both the front and the garden elevations have bay windows on the ground floor with sashes used extensively. The horizontal lines of the house are emphasized by ground floor extensions at each end of the main house; to the east is a courtyard surrounded by utility rooms and to the west a single storey outlier that did not feature on the original design but which is almost certainly contemporary with the original build. Unusual features, though not for Falkner, are the main staircase passing directly across one of the front windows and on both gable groups, the fine lead guttering which crosses from one roof valley to the other, directly across the central gable. A fine house, perfectly in tune with its surroundings and its garden.

In a completely different style was Leigh House also

Leigh House, Farnham

designed around 1906. Where Mavins Court is reserved, with just the occasional flashiness, Leigh House, in full-blown Queen Anne style is wonderfully exuberant. Broad stuccoed pilasters break up the front and rear elevations, drawing the eye upwards to the sweeping tiled expanse of roof pierced by hipped dormers and surmounted by elegant chimneys. The entrance front is symmetrically laid out around a grand portico that reaches to the roof and terminates in a segmental pediment. This arrangement is almost mirrored in the rear façade but here the portico has a broken pediment and above the rear door to the garden is a round, square paned, window with a surround of moulded fruit and vegetables. As at Mavins Court, Falkner has again used darker headers dispersed through the red brick of the elevations to avoid monotony and has followed his trick of leading the main staircase across the front windows. All in all, an impressive house, sensibly laid out, stoutly built and at peace in its garden.

During the years leading up to the First World War a number of estates had been built in Farnham and Falkner was busy designing many houses for them. At the same time he was also working on various projects within the town centre often in association with Charles Ernest Borelli, several of which were concerned with the preservation or restoration of existing buildings within the town, for example the Goats Head Inn purchased by Borelli in 1910 and carefully restored over several years. But with the Great War both Falkner and Borelli enlisted in the armed forces with Falkner first enlisting in the Royal Engineers within months of the outbreak of hostilities. However, the following year, a motorcycle accident leading to a serious leg injury and subsequent blood poisoning, put him out of the war and left him with a permanent limp, though this did not prevent him gaining a commission as second lieutenant in the reorganised Royal Flying Corps in 1918. With the Armistice, Falkner returned to his beloved Farnham to continue his work; housing schemes at Hale for the local council, which exercised his ability to work to a tight budget contrasting with work on the Great Austins Estate where the requirement for quality houses for the fiscally endowed posed less of a problem.

Farnham Town Hall

Notwithstanding his disastrous partnership with David Niven before the war, in the late 1920s Falkner entered a partnership with another Farnham architect Guy Maxwell Aylwin. This collaboration proved to be much more successful with a number of high quality buildings being designed including the Town Hall and associated buildings begun in 1930. Also during this period Falkner submitted a design to the 1931 competition for a new cathedral for Guildford, coming tenth out of 280 submissions.

This ambitious Town Hall project, that first saw the light of day in 1929, was to lead to the major redevelopment of the very heart of the town and involved the demolition of the Victorian Town Hall and Corn Exchange of 1865-6 by E. Wyndham Tarn. It is a truism to say that this earlier building in an exuberant and colourful Neo-Gothic was unloved by Farnhamians and its replacement by something more in keeping inevitable. While it made perfect sense to give the design to Falkner (and that was apparently always Borelli's plan according to Falkner) in the event the project leadership was given to a Birmingham architect T.W. Benslyn with

Falkner and Aylwin as assistants. Falkner later claimed that, "in all respects…the design was mine – Benslyn's role being to eat the Directors' dinners and soften them up."

The eventual design, which also incorporated the Bailiffs Hall and the vestigial Conduit, was another neo-Georgian composition which was unveiled in stages between 1931 and 1935. The two storey design which comprised the entire corner of Castle Street and The Borough, was fronted by a colonnade, necessary to accommodate the offices of the Inland Revenue on the first floor, and which formed an arcade at street level containing a row of shops. When Falkner came to the restoration of the Bailiffs Hall and its inclusion in his composition he faced several problems, not least of which was the fact that the original façade had been destroyed when the hall was chopped back in the last century. A search for illustrations of that frontage failed to turn up anything of significance and so the present front is entirely Falkner's and a very credible job he made of it.

The Town Hall buildings incorporated part of an earlier

Overdeans Court, Dippenhall

structure that stood on the adjacent site. Knights Bank in Castle Street, a Norman Shaw composition was threatened with demolition in 1931, a course of action to which Falkner had strongly objected. Unable to save the building, he salvaged the chimneys by incorporating them into the new Town Hall and The Bush Hotel. Generally the design won praise - this building and the rebuilt Lloyds Bank next door being deemed more suited to the Georgian architecture of Castle Street - though the loss of a hall for public functions, one of the Corn Exchange's uses, was commented on.

As Falkner's tally of building designs for Farnham mounted, and at times it seemed that there were few buildings in the town that he had not altered, reconstructed or built anew, one could have been forgiven for thinking that he was Farnham's favourite architect. That some had reservations about him as an architect and as a man seems evident from contemporary accounts, not least the Town Hall business. George Sturt, one of Farnham's sons and writer on its earlier social history, was very unhappy with Falkner's reinvention of Farnham's past, calling him, "...the evil genius of the countryside." "The

road yesterday, lovely to be sure, gave glimpses of the old delicious pathway he (Falkner) had helped to shut us out from and to spoil." In 1923 a Miss Paget presented the town with an ornate horse trough designed by Falkner but, "rejected by the unanimous disapproval of the town...(it)...still languished somewhere in a council yard." But if nothing else, Falkner was one of Farnham's "characters", taking great delight in being considered an English eccentric. And as time went by and Falkner aged his eccentricities increased with dress and house becoming increasingly shabby; one child remembering him as "...grey – he had grey hair and a full grey beard...wore grey clothes and drove a grey car."

With the approach of middle age Falkner's work on neo-Georgian Farnham gradually began to diminish while his architectural experiments in Dippenhall took up more and more of his time. Throughout his life Falkner had worked within the constraints imposed by the decision to concentrate on neo-Classical or neo-Georgian architectural forms (though it was not unknown for him to design

Grovers Farm, Dippenhall

occasionally in a stiff Shawesque Elizabethan). With the onset of middle age, there may have been a realization that neo-Georgian architecture with its strict rules of form would never allow him the freedom to express his artistic temperament in architecture. Whatever the reason, from 1921 onwards Falkner began a series of architectural experiments, producing buildings that were as far removed from his conventional work in Farnham as was possible, in a style that Nairn and Pevsner described as "whimsical free-Tudor vernacular." From this time too, Falkner's refusal to abide by the regulations that govern all building work became more apparent with constant disagreements with the local authority.

His first project at Dippenhall was the purchase of Deans Farm in 1921 to which he made extensive alterations and which became Dippenhall Grange, and the conversion of a cottage in the grounds into a house called Deans. Then, using a barn dismantled from nearby, he produced The Barn, a long low whale-back roofed structure which featured a two storey bay window lighting the central hall. The practice of integrating redundant farm buildings into his houses now became a feature of his work at Dippenhall and his next house, Overdeans Court, started in 1926 incorporated not only barns, but a cowstall and a stable. This was followed by Baldridges (later called Meads), and Halfway House in 1930. Next came Burles, regarded as one of his finest houses, constructed of two barns end to end and a granary. Burles was followed by Burles Lodge, begun in 1955. His last two projects were Grovers Farm and Black Barn, which was unfinished at his death. It may be that the death of his friend and sole assistant, Alfred Hack, in an accident while working on Black Barn caused Falkner to lose interest in the project.

For Falkner, Dippenhall was experimental architecture. It allowed him to concentrate on pure design without the distraction of client or regulation. And while the result was sublime artistically, it was often a disaster structurally.

Overdeans Court has been likened to a rambling mediaeval village street; it is long and thin, being only one room wide throughout. A former barn terminates the house at each end, these being set at a slight angle to each other with the remaining space between them reputedly filled with other outbuildings. The resulting elevations of mixed stone at ground floor level and timber frame up to the eaves are a triumph, producing an accretive design that could easily be several hundred years old (as indeed the frames probably are). Falkner's habit of incorporating architectural odds and ends from other houses merely enhances this effect.

In contrast to his vernacular work at Overdeans Court which was effectively a completely new building, Grovers Farm nearby began life as a farmworkers cottage fronting a pair of oast houses, a relic of Farnham's rich hop growing heritage. Falkner took the frontage and "Georgified" it by squaring off the elevation and adding a classical doorcase, ornate cornice and parapet. Then at the rear, the distinctive oast flues were removed and the kilns reroofed with a patent lightweight concrete mix of his own invention. The resulting room was then connected to the main house by knocking through a doorway and adding a fireplace, the flue of which consisted of an old copper with the bottom knocked out and lengths of land drain that wound up through the house to emerge on the roof! To complete the roof structure where the elevation had been built up, an oversized barn like roof was added at right angles to the main roof, its large dimensions resulting in a substantial bracketed overhang to the rear.

By 1963 a total of nine buildings had been completed or started at Dippenhall. The artistic freedom and sheer imagination that Falkner could never display in his town centre work was given full rein here in house after house, many incorporating examples of his wood carving skills and all built with a total disregard for inconvenient architectural regulation. But that same disregard for regulation was nearly the coup-de-grace for his work at Dippenhall. Unable to sell the houses, Falkner was in the habit of letting them and then failing to carry out necessary maintenance. The result was that within a few years of his death, the properties were in dire need of expensive and extensive renovation and several were semi-derelict before being saved by sympathetic owners. Black Barn could not be saved and was demolished.

With his death in 1963 the Dippenhall experiment came to an end. In a sense, his life had ended, as it should have begun – at Dippenhall. Farnham lost one of its leading figures and its greatest architect. During his rich life Falkner had been the architect for over 100 buildings in the Farnham area. His concern for the protection of the town's older buildings had born fruit in his own day and would go on to inspire Farnham people with a love for their town and its buildings.

There is however an irony in this, in that Falkner's work in Farnham verged at times on fakery, to such a degree that nothing in architectural terms can be taken for granted in the town centre. Yet Falkner always had his eye on "the big picture", on the sympathetic grouping of buildings, and so perhaps can be forgiven his historical *fixes*.

Falkner's Buildings:

Due to the number of buildings involved, the reader is directed to the appendix.

Appendix

This inevitably incomplete survey covers an area roughly coterminous with the administrative Borough of Waverley though some entries fall outside of this boundary. The survey is arranged alphabetically by principal town and civil parish and where a building falls outside the Borough boundary, it is appended to the nearest town or parish. It is recognized that the survey is incomplete and, while every effort has been taken to ensure accuracy, it is inevitable that some errors will have crept in. However it is hoped that it may provide a starting point on the road to a more complete architectural record of the period that will grow as more information becomes available.

Although most buildings are extant, the survey includes some which have been lost where it is felt that their inclusion is merited for historical or architectural reasons. Buildings which carry either local or national listing are denoted by an asterisk*.

The reader is once again reminded that the majority of buildings featured are in private hands and that the privacy of the owners should be respected at all times.

Building	Architect	Date	Notes
Bramley Parish			
Snowdenham Hall* Snowdenham Lane	Ralph Nevill J Bentley	1886-7	Built for the Courage family Addition of Great Hall possibly built 1868 with additions in 1886
Millmead House* Snowdenham Lane	Edwin Lutyens	1904-7	Built for Jekyll, Jekyll garden
Garden House* at Millmead House Snowdenham Lane	Edwin Lutyens	1904-7	Built for Jekyll
Church of St. Andrew* Horsham Road, Grafham	Henry Woodyer	1861-4	Built at his own expense, he is buried in The Churchyard
Lych gate to Church* Horsham Road, Grafham	Henry Woodyer	1861-4	
Grafham Grange* Horsham Road, Grafham	Henry Woodyer AB Burnell Shepherd	1854 1871 1893 & 1906	Built for himself Additions Extensions Addition of billiard room
Orchards* Munstead Heath Road	Edwin Lutyens Edwin Lutyens	1896-9 1909, 1914	Lutyens first major work. Built for Sir William & Lady Chance Additions - Jekyll garden- Builder - Thomas Underwood of Dunsfold
Holy Trinity Church High Street	Henry Woodyer	1850, 1876	Restoration
Busbridge Parish			
High Barn*	Sir Robert Lorimer Walter Godfrey	1902 1926	Built for Hon Stuart Pladell Bouverie Additions
High Hascombe* Hascombe Court Road	Edwin Lutyens	1896-7 1903	Built for CA Cook Addition of music room by Lutyens Built as Sullingstead

Building	Architect	Date	Notes
Munstead Place* Heath Lane	Edwin Lutyens	1891-2	Built for CD Heatley with lodge Built as Munstead Corner-Jekyll garden
Munstead Wood* Heath Lane	Edwin Lutyens	1896-7	Built for Jekyll Builder - Thomas Underwood of Dunsfold
Munstead House* Munstead Heath Road	J J Stevenson Edwin Lutyens	1877-8 1903	Built for Jekyll & her mother. Remodelled by Lutyens to include an orangery which was rebuilt in 1969
Little Munstead* North Munstead Lane	Edwin Lutyens	1896-8	Built for Jekyll
The Hollies* & **Fir Tree Cottage*** North Munstead Lane	Edwin Lutyens	1895	Semi-detached Cottages
North Munstead* North Munstead Lane	Harold Falkner	c.1920	Virtual rebuild of 16th century house
Water Tower* Munstead Heath Road	Elspeth Beard	late 19th c.	Conversion by architect owner

Chiddingfold Parish

Building	Architect	Date	Notes
Pickhurst*	J M Brydon	1883/5	Built for himself
Pickhurst Stable Court*	J M Brydon	1885	
Pickhurst Lodge*	J M Brydon	1885	
Church of St. Mary	Henry Woodyer	1869	Restoration
Tower House The Nipp	John Monk	1980s	

Cranleigh Parish

Building	Architect	Date	Notes
Church of St. Nicolas Church Lane	William Butterfield? Henry Woodyer	1845 1861-8	First restoration Second restoration
Rectory High Street	Henry Woodyer Manning, Clamp & Partners	1863 1987	Additions to rear

Building	Architect	Date	Notes
Lych gate to Church* Church Lane	Henry Woodyer	1880	Some authorities ascribe to Street
Cranleigh School* Horseshoe Lane	Henry Woodyer	1864-5	
Chapel*	Henry Woodyer	1867	
Connaught Building	Sir Edwin Cooper	1926-9	
NW gateway to Baynards* Horsham Road	Thomas Rickman or Matthew Digby Wyatt	1850-60	
Baynards Lodge* Horsham Road	Thomas Rickman or Matthew Digby Wyatt	1850-60	
Cranleigh Arts Centre High Street	Sampson, Kempthorne Andrew Edwards	1847 1871	C of E School till 1965 Additions
Post Office High Street	GAH Pearce	1959	Built for Ministry of Works
Stocklund Square High Street	Covell, Matthews & Partners	1966-8	Built on site of railway station & goods yard
Park Mead Estate Ewhurst Road	Highet & Phillips	1963-7	
Park Mead Schools Park Drive	Barber, Bundy & Greenfield & County architect's dept.	1966-7 1967-8	
Wyphurst Amlets Lane	Reginald Blomfield	1871 1907	Built for Chadwick-Healey family Additions
Alderbrook	Richard Norman Shaw	1881	Demolished post WW2 and new house built 1960s. Originally built for Pandali Ralli
Baltic House The Common	Thomas Wade	1926	Built by Warrens
Flagstones Horsham Road	William Sydie Dakers	1924	Built for Dr. JK Willis

Building	Architect	Date	Notes
Police Station Horsham Road	Frank Howell	1902	County Architect Son of Charles Henry Howell
Library High Street	County Architects Department.	1985	
Lady Peake Institute Church Lane	Henry Peake	1881?	

Dunsfold Parish

Building	Architect	Date	Notes
Bowbricks	Thomas Underwood	c.1840?	Lutyens builder

Elstead Parish

Building	Architect	Date	Notes
Church of St James* Westbrook Hill	Garling	1871	Restoration
Fulbrook House* Fulbrook Lane	Edwin Lutyens Roderick Gradidge	1896-9 1970s 1980s	Built for Mr & Mrs Gerald Streatfield Extended and Altered
Lodge and Store* NE of Fulbrook House	Edwin Lutyens	1897	
Charles Hill Court	Detmar Blow Stedman & Blower		Alterations

Ewhurst Parish

Building	Architect	Date	Notes
Lukyns* Three Mile Road	Ernest Newton	1911	Jekyll garden
Long Copse* Pitch Hill Road	Alfred Powell	1897	Arts & Crafts House built for Mrs Mudie-Cooke
Cottage at Long Copse* Pitch Hill Road	Alfred Powell	1897	
Coneyhurst on the Hill* **Mendip & Brackenlea*** Pitch Hill Road	Phillip Webb	1884-6	Built for Mary Ann Ewart

Building	Architect	Date	Notes
High Raise Pitch Hill Road	Philip Webb	1886	Former stables for Coneyhurst Built by William & George King of Abinger Hammer
Hurtwood Edge* The Warren	Arthur Bolton	1910	
Marylands* Shere Road	Oliver Hill	1928-9	
Woolpit* (Duke of Kent's School) Peaslake Road	E George & Peto	1886-8	Built for Sir Henry Doulton
Baynards Horsham Road *Surviving elements include* **Clock Tower*** **Gatehouse and walling*** **Stable entrance***, **Courtyard and wall**	Thomas Rickman Thomas Rickman Thomas Rickman Thomas Rickman	c.1834-38 c.1840 c.1840 c.1840	Extensive rebuild of earlier House For Rev. Thomas Thurlow. Possible later remodelling by Sir Matthew Digby Wyatt. Benjamin Ferrey also did some work here. Largely destroyed by fire 1979
Church of St. Peter & Paul **Tower**	Robert Ebbels	1838	Rebuild after original tower collapsed
Summerfold	Richard Osbourne? Michael Wilson	1910 1980s	 Full restoration
Copse Hill	Christopher Turnor	1905	
Hurtwood House Holmbury St Mary	Christopher Turnor	1908	
Lilyfields	RA Briggs	c.1900	"Bungalow Briggs"
Moonhall	GL Kennedy	1920	Remodelled 1937
North Breache Manor	Sir Aston Webb		
High Wykehurst	Ernest Newton	1906-7	Built for Prof. William Frecheville
Coverwood Peaslake	Gerald C Horsley	1909	Built for Michael Stephens

Building	Architect	Date	Notes
Ellens Ellens Green	Maurice Webb	1914	Extensive rebuild of earlier house For Frederick Warburg
Holmdale Holmbury St. Mary	George E Street	1875	This was Street's own house

Farnham

Building	Architect	Date	Notes
1-5 Town Hall Buildings* The Borough	G Maxwell Aylwin Harold Falkner W T Benslyn	1930-4	
6 Town Hall Buildings* **(Bailiffs Hall & Arcade)**	Harold Falkner	1930-5	Rebuild of c.17th building
6&7 The Borough	Horace Field	post 1915	Reconstruction
38&39 The Borough*	 Cheston	1865 1904	3 eastern bays 2 western bays, reconstructed
40 The Borough	Harold Falkner	1911	Restoration
The Bush Hotel* The Borough	 Harold Falkner & G Maxwell Aylwin	c.1840 1931	Alterations to earlier building Alterations to ground floor
Goats Head Inn The Borough	Harold Falkner	1910	Purchased by Borelli who restored it with Harold Falkner. Ceased trading in 1909 & became a shop called the Spinning Wheel
Barclays Bank The Borough	AJ & LR Stedman Stedman & Blower	1930-31 1970	Converted from bakers Alterations
LH Smith, Hairdresser The Borough	AJ & LR Stedman	1930s	Altered in 1950s
Borelli Mews/Yard Off the Borough	Broadway & Malyan	c.1980s	
Guildford House Castle Street	CV Tillett Stedman & Blower	1961 2000	Restoration Conservatory added to rear elevation

Building	Architect	Date	Notes
49 Castle Street*	Falkner & Stedman	1929	Addition of modern front
61 Castle Street	LR Stedman	1930s	For Dr Ealand, Cottage conversion
Lloyds Bank* (75 Castle Street)	Guy Dawber & Wilson	1931	
Hill House Castle Hill	Harold Falkner		
Cherry Trees Castle Hill	Stedman & Blower		For Groocock
St George's Mews Off Castle Street	Broadway & Malyan	c.1980s	
1&2 Church Passage*	Colston of Winchester	1860	
Clockhouse Dogflud Way	Broadway & Malyan	c.1980s	
Riverside Court Off Dogflud Way	Arthur Gomez	1980s	Scheme by Waverley Architects Dept.
Farnham Sports Centre Dogflud Way	Arthur Gomez	1980s	Scheme by Waverley Architects Dept.
Victoria Garden Arch Brightwells Road	Harold Falkner / Stedman & Blower	1897 / 1997	Originally swimming pool entrance / Conservation of arch
Royal Deer Buildings South Street	AJ & LR Stedman	1929	
The Liberal Club* South Street	Edwin Lutyens	1895	
Waverley Borough Council Locality Office* South Street	Paxton Hood Watson	1901 / 1956	Alterations
Solicitors' Offices 11 South Street	Arthur J Stedman	1912?	Now Bells Potter

Building	Architect	Date	Notes
Farnham Central Club* 13 South Street	Paxton Hood Watson	1891	Was Working Mens Institute
Architects Offices for AJ Stedman 36 South Street	Arthur J Stedman	1908	Demolished 1980
United Reformed Church South Street	Thomas Wonnacott		
Falkner Court Off South Street	Arthur Gomez	1980s	Scheme by Waverley Architects Dept.
7 West Street	JA Eggar	early 20th c.	
20 West Street	John Kingham	1930	Alterations
6 West Street* (6&6a West Street)	Harold Falkner?	19th c.	Reconstruction?
Adult Education Centre* 25 West Street	Paxton Hood Watson	1872 1895	Former Grammar School
104a West Street*	Harold Falkner	1951	Early to mid 19th c. building reconstructed by Falkner
98-99 West Street	AJ&LR Stedman	1936	
1-8 McDonalds Almshouses* West Street	AJ Stedman	1905	
Old Cemetery Lodge* West Street	Stedman & Blower	1870 1970s	Alterations & improvements
Farnham Library Vernon House Extension West Street	County Architects Dept.	1990	
Alliance House West Street	Harold Falkner & G Maxwell Aylwin	c.1930	Reconstruction as partnership
Wykeham House 40 West Street	Harold Falkner	post1927	Reconstruction

Building	Architect	Date	Notes
112 West Street	G Maxwell Aylwin	c.1950	Reconstructed frontage
113 West Street	John Kingham	c.1921	Reconstruction
114&115 West Street	Harold Falkner	c.1952	Reconstruction
Sampsons Alms House West Street	Harold Falkner AJ Stedman	1933-4	Alterations
Alywards Wine Shop West Street	AJ&LR Stedman	1930s	
Maritime House West Street	G Maxwell Aylwin	mid 1930s	
96-97 West Street	G Maxwell Aylwin	1968	Office block replaced Butchers shop & book shop
St Andrews School West Street	Colston AJ&LR Stedman	1860 post 1945	New School hall
8&8a East Street	Stedman & Blower	1974	Above arcade, alterations
The Marlborough Head 14 East Street	John Howard	1929	Reconstruction
86-87 East Street	AJ&LR Stedman	post 1945	HC Patrick, Funeral Showroom
94&95 East Street	Harold Falkner	20th c.	Reconstruction
Seven Stars PH	Harold Falkner	1929-30	With GM Aylwin
Electric Theatre East Street	Harold Falkner		Demolished
Swain & Jones Garage East Street	HY Margary		Was Swain & Clowes
Gas Showrooms East Street	AJ&LR Stedman	1930s	Demolished by Woolmead
Church of St James* East Street	Henry Woodyer Roy Toms	1876 1980s	Converted to flats

Building	Architect	Date	Notes
3 Coopers Terrace East Street	Stedman & Blower	1970s?	Alterations
Health Centre South of East Street	County Architects Dept.	1967-8	
Eastgate East Street	Broadway & Malyan	c.1880s	
Chestnuts East Street	Broadway & Malyan Harold Falkner	c.1880s 1921	Old Labour Exchange Minor alterations
Former St Polycarps School Bear Lane	G Bulbeck	1896	Demolished
The Exchange PH* Station Hill	Harold Falkner & G Maxwell Aylwin	mid 19thc. 1929	Was The Railway Arms, then Railway Hotel, then Blue Boy, then Exchange 1999. Additions & alterations
Church of England Schools* Upper Church Lane	Colston of Winchester	1860	
St Marks Church	Benjamin Ferrey	1844	
Grammar School Morley Road	Jarvis & Richards	1906	County Architects
Stream Cottage 41 Ford Lane, Shortheath	Harold Falkner		Reconstruction Falkner lived here 1911-27
Elm Tree Cottage 10 Great Austins	Harold Falkner	1909-10	For Frank Leonard Borelli Brother of Charles Ernest
Furzedown 17 Great Austins	Harold Falkner	c.1911	
The Mount 19 Great Austins	Harold Falkner		
Farlands Croft 20 Great Austins	Harold Falkner	1922	

Building	Architect	Date	Notes
Sussex House 24 Great Austins	Harold Falkner		
Orchard House 7 Little Austins Road	Harold Falkner Stedman & Blower	1904 1974	Alterations
The Beeches 1 Little Austins Road	Harold Falkner		
Little Austins House 4 Little Austins Road	Harold Falkner	1905	
Leigh House 10 Little Austins Road	Harold Falkner		
Roffey 2 Middle Avenue	Harold Falkner		
6 Middle Avenue	Harold Falkner		
9 Middle Avenue	Harold Falkner		
Sherwood 14 Middle Avenue	Harold Falkner		
2 Greenhill Road* (Mavins End & Mavins House)	Harold Falkner	1927 1981	Subdivided
Montclare House* 10 Greenhill Road	Harold Falkner	1908	For RC Ratcliffe
Ilona Greenhill Road	Harold Falkner		
Mavins Court* 4 Greenhill Road	Harold Falkner	1906	
Marlingford 7 Greenhill Road	Harold Falkner		
Tilford Way 11 Greenhill Road	Harold Falkner		Divided

Building	Architect	Date	Notes
Delvern House 13 Greenhill Road	Harold Falkner	1905	
Greenhill Farm 20 Greenhill Road	Harold Falkner		Barn conversion & reconstruction
Crowhamhurst Lancaster Avenue	Harold Falkner		
Squirrels 5 Old Farnham Lane	Harold Falkner		
Firgrove House 47 Old Farnham Lane	Harold Falkner		
The Priory 6 Swingate Road	Harold Falkner	1932	
Shottisham Lodge 7 Swingate Road	Harold Falkner	1906	Bourne Corner
Cobbetts 1 Mavins Road	Harold Falkner	pre 1914	
Vine Cottage 5 Old Church Lane	Harold Falkner		Porch
Leigh House 1 Leigh Lane	Harold Falkner	1906-8	
Sands Lodge 2 Leigh Lane	Harold Falkner	1906-8	
Leigh Cottage 3 Leigh Lane	Harold Falkner	1906-8	
Sands Cottage 4 Leigh Lane	Harold Falkner	1906-8	
Greenhill Brow 11 Leigh Lane	Harold Falkner	1911	

Building	Architect	Date	Notes
Green Tubs 6 Packway	Harold Falkner	1923	
Strangers Corner 88 Tilford Road	Harold Falkner	1897	
Great Austins House 90 Tilford Road	Harold Falkner		
Buckland House/Fairywood 92 Tilford Road	Harold Falkner	1911	Divided
Robin Hey Tilford Road	Harold Falkner	1911	
Blue Cedars Tilford Road	Harold Falkner		
The Corner 80 Tilford Road	Arthur J Stedman	1900s?	Later AJ Stedman's house
Headons Cottage Off Tilford Road	Harold Falkner		
Waverley Arms PH Waverley Lane	Harold Falkner & G Maxwell Aylwin	1931	New building on site of earlier PH
Over Compton 55 Waverley Lane	Harold Falkner		
Costleys Waverley Lane	Harold Falkner		Now demolished?
Gwanda 12 Old Compton Lane	Harold Falkner		
Compton Hill House 14 Old Compton Lane	Harold Falkner		
Sentry Hill Compton Way	Harold Falkner		

Building	Architect	Date	Notes
The Croft Compton Way	Harold Falkner		
Frensham Compton Way	Harold Falkner		
Delarden House Compton Way	Harold Falkner	Late 1930	
90 Weydon Hill Road	Harold Falkner		
92 Weydon Hill Road	Harold Falkner		
Rowan Tree Cottage 1 Ridgeway Hill Road	Harold Falkner		
3 Ridgeway Hill Road	Harold Falkner		
5 Ridgeway Hill Road	Harold Falkner		
40 Ridgeway Road	Harold Falkner		
42 Ridgeway Road	Harold Falkner		
44 Ridgeway Road	Harold Falkner		
46 Ridgeway Road	Harold Falkner		
64 Ridgeway Road	Harold Falkner		
2 Searle Road	Harold Falkner		
3 Searle Road	Harold Falkner		
Searle House 56 Firgrove Hill Road	Harold Falkner		Rebuilt after flying bomb damage
70 Firgrove Hill Road	Harold Falkner		
Lodge Hill House Lodge Hill Road	Harold Falkner	1903?	

Building	Architect	Date	Notes
Gold Hill Place Gold Hill Road	Harold Falkner		Divided
Hart Brown Solicitors 17 Victoria Street	Harold Falkner		
17 West End Grove	Harold Falkner		For Mr Sturt
Knole House Old Park Lane	Harold Falkner		
Jolly Farmer PH Runfold	Harold Falkner	1927-30	With GM Aylwin
Camelia Lodge Longdown Road	Curtis W Green	c.1910	
Longdown Longdown Road	Curtis W Green	c.1910	
Farnham Police Station Long Bridge	John Harrison	1963	
Trimmers Cottage Hospital Menin Way	HY Margary		Now Phyllis Tuckwell Hospice
Isolation Hospital Green Lane	HY Margary		
Regal Cinema	Scott	1933	Demolished
West Mead The Hart	John Spratley & Partners		
Pightile House The Sands	Arthur J Stedman		Present to RCPA
Church House Union Road	Richard Bassnett Preston	1909	
Garage/Workshops Union Road	Arthur J Stedman	1910?	Demolished 1960s

Building	Architect	Date	Notes
St Peters C of E Aided School Wrecclesham	AJ&LR Stedman	post 1945	New school hall
Chafyn Grove School	AJ&LR Stedman	post 1945	New chapel & science labs
New Rectory Wrecclesham	AJ&LR Stedman	post 1945	
3 Downing Street	AJ&LR Stedman	post 1945	Alterations for Wey Valley Water Co. Offices
22 Downing Street	G Maxwell Aylwin	1949	Reconstruction
37&38 Downing Street	G Maxwell Aylwin	1950	Alterations to earlier house
The Memorial Hall	AJ&LR Stedman		Internal alterations
Tanyard Cottages Maltings	Stedman & Blower	1984	Internal rebuild, renew extension
New Ashgate Gallery Lower Church Lane	Stedman & Blower	1987	
31&31a Lower Church Lane	Stedman & Blower	1995	Rebuilt to form two residences
Hall Grove School	Stedman & Blower	post 1945	New wing & hall
Leightons Downing Street	Stedman & Blower	1968	Conversion, was Hammicks
Health Centre	Stedman & Blower	post 1945	Alterations
Magistrates Court Union Road	Stedman & Blower	2000	New court & alterations Converted
Grange Cottage Old Park Lane	Stedman & Blower		Built for Col Johnson
Surrey Institute of Art & Design Falkner Road	County Architects Dept	1969	

Building	Architect	Date	Notes
SIAD Studio Block, Library & Resource Centre Falkner Road	Nick Evans	1996	
SIAD Student Village Falkner Road	Nick Evans	1997	
Retirement Homes Opposite SIAD	County Architects Dept.	1967-9	
Shepherds Court Sheephouse	Roy Toms	1980s	
The Millennium Centre Crosby Way	John Monk	1997-9	Monk worked for the Hawarth King Partnership in Farnham
St Joan of Arc RC Church Tilford Road	John Edward Dixon-Spain	1923	
Church of St Thomas The Bourne	H Sidebotham & Sir C Nicholson	1911	
Dippenhall Grange* Dippenhall Road, Dippenhall	Harold Falkner	1921	Was Deans Farm
Deans Knowe* Dippenhall	Harold Falkner	1921	Additions to earlier house
The Barn* Dippenhall Road, Dippenhall	Harold Falkner	1921	Listed as 1925
Overdeans Court* Dippenhall Road, Dippenhall	Harold Falkner	1925	
Meads* Doras Green Lane, Dippenhall	Harold Falkner	1930	Was Baldridges
Halfway House Doras Green Lane, Dippenhall	Harold Falkner	1930s	Originally the lodge for Meads
Burles & Burles Cottage* Lower Old Park, Dippenhall	Harold Falkner	1937 1999	Repairs

Building	Architect	Date	Notes
Burles Lodge Off Crondall Lane, Dippenhall	Harold Falkner	post 1955	
Grovers Farm Runwick Lane, Dippenhall	Harold Falkner	1958	
Black Barn (or Old Barn) Runwick Lane, Dippenhall	Harold Falkner	post 1963	Demolished
Ridgeway House Dippenhall	Stedman & Blower	1968	Built for Kingham
Two Chapels & Lodge **Hale Cemetery** Alma Lane, Upper Hale	Sidney Stapley	1872	
1-3 Portland Terrace Hale Road	Stedman & Blower	1991	Alterations
Ravenswood Hale Road	Stedman & Blower	1971	Built for Kenchington
Upper Hale Primary School Alma Lane	County Architects Dept. County Architect's Dept.	1967-8 1989-90	Additions to earlier school New hall
Heath End Secondary School Hale Reeds	County Architects Dept.	1966-8	
The Dial House Shortfield Common	Harold Falkner		Barn conversion/reconstruction
Bungalows Shortfields	Stedman & Blower	post 1945	Farnham RDC
Church of St John Old Kiln Lane, Churt	Ewan Christian	1868	
Churt Place or Bron-y-de Thursley Road, Churt	Philip Tilden	1921	For Lloyd George
2 The Chase Farnham Road, Churt	Harold Falkner		

Building	Architect	Date	Notes
Barford Mill Off Kitts Lane, Churt	Stedman & Blower	1978	For Lanler, alterations?

Frensham Parish

Building	Architect	Date	Notes
Pierrepont* Frensham Road	Richard Norman Shaw	1876-8	Built for Richard Henry Combe around older house
Stable Block &The Court * Pierrepont, Frensham Road	H T Keates	1888	Altered/extended in 20th c.
Pierrepont Lodge* Frensham Road	Richard Norman Shaw	1876-8	For Richard Henry Combe
The Hop House* Kennel Lane	Richard Norman Shaw	1870	Restored in 20th c.
Lowicks House* Sandy Lane	CFA Voysey	1894	Built for FJ Horniman Extended & altered 1898, 1904,1907 & 1911 by Voysey
Church of St. Mary	Hahn	1868	
Church of St. Mary Tower	WD Caroe	1929	Restored
Frensham Heights School	Mr Waller	1900	
Shortfield House	Chuter	c.1885	
Cottages	Edwin Lutyens	1891	
Great Holt	Edwin Lutyens	1902	Alterations for Major Boyce Combe
Sentry Hill Frensham Common	Harold Falkner		House & cottage
The Grange	Arthur J Stedman		

Godalming

Building	Architect	Date	Notes
Ladywell Convent* Ashstead Lane	Sir Guy Dawber	1910	Built for Major-General DA Scott As Tuesley Court.
		1956	Converted to convent 1956
	G Clay & Partners	1960s	Additions 1960s

Building	Architect	Date	Notes
Gate Lodge to above*	Sir Guy Dawber	1910	
Garage and two Cottages*At above	Sir Guy Dawber	1910	
Grammar School Tuesley Lane	County Architects Dept.	1926-30 1950s-1990	Various additions
Science Block	Atkins, Lister & Drew	1995	
The Thunder House* Heath Lane	Edwin Lutyens	1895	For Jekyll
The Quadrangle* Heath Lane	Edwin Lutyens	1891&1901 1950s	Former potting sheds & outbuildings to Munstead Wood. Converted to house in 1950s
Munstead Orchard* Brighton Road	Edwin Lutyens	1898-9	For Jekyll
Munstead Wood Hut Brighton Road	Edwin Lutyens	1894-5	Built as The Hut for Jekyll
Munstead Grange Alldens Lane	EW Mountford	1902	
Stilemans Heath Road	Nicholson & Corlette	1909	
Munstead Oaks	EJ May	1905	
Church of St John the Baptist* Brighton Road	George Gilbert Scott jun.	1865-7	For John & Emma Ramsden. Chancel Screen by Lutyens 1899. Jekyll Memorial in churchyard. Windows by Burne Jones, made up by Morris & Co. Nave windows by AR Nicholson
Busbridge Hall	George & Yates	1906	
St Hilarys School Holloway Hill	Stedman & Blower	post 1945	Library, dining room & classrooms
Church of St. Edmund* **King & Martyr** Croft Road	FA Walters	1905/6	

Building	Architect	Date	Notes
Municipal Offices & Borough Hall Bridge Street	JH Norris	1906/8	Norris was Borough Surveyor
Police Station & Accommodation Block Wharf Street	County Architects Dept.	1966-8	
Terraced Houses Pound Close	JM Ramsay	1958	
Congregational Church and Sunday School* Bridge Street/The Burys	Welman & Street	1868 1883 20th c.	Alterations
Godalming United Church Bridge Street	Gordon & Gumpton	1903	Originally the Hugh Price Hughs Memorial Church
Church of St. Peter & Paul Church Street	Ralph Neville & Sir GG Scott	1877-9	Restoration
Library Bridge Street	County Architects Dept.	1955-60?	
Phillips Memorial Cloister* Borough Road	H Thackeray Turner Gertrude Jekyll	1913	With planting by Jekyll Alterations 1965, restoration 1986 Memorial to Jack Phillips SS Titanic wireless operator
Godalming Railway Station*	Sir William Tite?	1859	
Westbrook* Westbrook Road	H Thackeray Turner	1899-1900	Built for himself 20th c. Alterations Jekyll garden
Art School	James Dartford of GA Jellicoe & Partners	1958	
Red House Frith Hill Road	Edwin Lutyens	1897-9	For Rev WH Evans
Cliffhanger	Michael Manser Associates	1963	

Building	Architect	Date	Notes
Charterhouse School* Hurtmore Road	Philip C Hardwick	1872	
The Great Hall*	Sir Arthur Blomfield	1885	
South African Cloister*	WD Caroe	1901	
Memorial Chapel*	Sir Giles G Scott	1922-27	Modified Gothic with A&C detail
Brooke Hall & School	Douglas Stewart	1915	
Sergeant's Lodge* the Conference Store*	Edwin Lutyens	C.1893	Former dairy of Northbrook House
Seven Accommodation Blocks Inc. Heywood Court	Sir Giles Scott Son & Partner	1965-74	
School of Technology	Sir Giles Scott Son & Partner		
Dining Hall	Sir Giles Scott Son & Partner	1973 or 8?	
School of Music	Sir Giles Scott Son & Partner	1979-83	
Ben Travers Theatre	Sir Giles Scott Son & Partner	1979-83	
Monkswood Hurtmore	Forsyth & Maule	1912	
Norney Grange & Lodge Shackleford	CFA Voysey	1897 1903	Designed for Rev Leighton Grane Additions
Stable Lodge, Norney Shackleford	CFA Voysey?	1904	
Priorsfield School Priorsfield Road Hurtmore	CFA Voysey Tom Muntzer	1900 1904 2001	Additions Additions
North Cottages* Priorsfield Road, Hurtmore	CFA Voysey	1904	
Church of St. John the Evangelist Farncombe	Sir George Gilbert Scott CF Hayward	1847 1860 1875 1881	Additions
Farncombe School St Johns Street	Charles Henry Howell	1857	Now Farncombe Day Centre Later County Architect

Building	Architect	Date	Notes
Binscombe County First School	County Architects Dept	1982-3	
Wyatts Almshouses Meadrow	BW Ridley	1957-8	New cottage quadrangle added

Hambledon Parish

Building	Architect	Date	Notes
Feathercombe* Feathercombe Lane	Ernest Newton	1910	For Eric Parker
Tigbourne Cottage* Lane End	Edwin Lutyens	c.1899	
Little Leat* Lane End	Edwin Lutyens	c.1899	
Tigbourne Court* Petworth Road, Wormley	Edwin Lutyens Horace Farquarson	1899-01 1910	For Sir Edgar Horne. Billiard room added
Lower Vann* Vann Lane	Mr Pocock WD Caröe	1890 1908	Remodelled 16th c. house Barn conversion and new wing added
Goodbrook House Woodlands Road	WD Caröe	1910 1986	Conversion of 18th c. cottages and additions Further additions inc. new wing
Church of St Peter	Rev. Edward Bullock	1846	Rebuild
Hambledon Hurst Woodlands Road	CFA Voysey	1919	Major addition by Voysey to earlier house of 1895 for Mr & Mrs van Gruisen
Bryony Hill Malthouse Lane	Robert Falconer Macdonald	1891	House, lodge, stables & Cottages Built for Andrew Muir
Bryony Lodge Malthouse Lane	Robert Falconer Macdonald	1891	Built for Andrew Muir
Stone Cottage	Robert Falconer Macdonald		Additions to earlier Cottage For Andrew Muir
Hydon Wood House	Fred Rowntree	1910	

Building	Architect	Date	Notes
Court Farm Church Lane	Seeley & Paget	1933	Substantial alterations to 17th c. house for Mr & Mrs C Dowson
Hill Top Farm Rock Hill	Judith Ledeboer	c.1970	Alterations and additions to 17th c. house for herself
Cobblers Woodlands Road	Barbara Dent	1972	Additions to 18th c. house for Mrs V Woolley by Ms. Dent of Dent & Howland of Cranleigh
Little Court Malthouse Lane	Scott Brownrigg & Turner	c.1970	Built for Mr Chapman
Tigbourne Wood	Philip Mabley	1957 1961 1963 1975	Own house Extended Annexe added Extended
The Village Hall	John Borrowman jun.	1903	
The Almshouses	Mr H Moon	1907	
Rock Hill House Rock Hill	Lady Casson	1967	Commissioned by Mr & MrsSBrooksbank

Hascombe Parish

Building	Architect	Date	Notes
Sussex Lodges, Park Hatch* Dunsfold Road, Loxhill	Edwin Lutyens	1890	Built for Joseph Godman
Church of St. Peter* School Lane	Henry Woodyer	1864	Complete rebuild
Winkworth Farm* Heath Road	Edwin Lutyens JD Coleridge FW Troup	1895 C.1908 1914	Remodelling of earlier house and barn extended into house. Extensions to back of house. Internal remodelling
Hoe Farm House* Hoe Lane	Edwin Lutyens	1890	Additions to early house for Joseph Godman and once owned by Churchill

Building	Architect	Date	Notes
Whinfold	Sir Robert Lorimer	1897-8	Built for Robert Murray
	Sir Walter Tapper	1903	Additions
Hascombe Court	JD Coleridge	1906-7	
Highlybourne	Thomas Underwood		Lutyens builder
Winkworth Hanger	Thomas Underwood		Lutyens builder

Haslemere

Building	Architect	Date	Notes
Shepherds Down & Trevorrow* Hill Road	CFA Voysey?	c.1913	Formally one dwelling
Ormiston Lodge* Bunch Lane	Paxton Hood Watson Or EP Warren?	1910	Former lodge on Witley Park Estate
The White House* Haslemere Road Grayswood	Amyas Connell	1930	Concrete with steel windows (Modern Movement) Of Connell Ward & Lucas
Church of St. Bartholomew* Green	JW Penfold	1871	More or less rebuilt apart from Church tower
Church of St. Christopher* St Christopher Green, Weyhill	Charles Spooner	1901-2	Arts & Crafts design. Spooner was follower of Morris
Branksome Conference Centre* Hindhead Road	EJ May Edward Cullinan James Stirling	1901 1971-2 1971-2	Additions to earlier house. Alterations & Additions for Olivetti. Built as Hilders for Lord Aberconway
New Place* Farnham Lane	CFA Voysey Stedman & Blower	1897	For AMM Steehan, later known As Sir Arthur Methuan Alterations?
New Place Cottage* Farnham Lane	CFA Voysey	1904	
Ballindune & Ballindune* Cottage	EJ May	1905	Built for Mr Gutteridge

Building	Architect	Date	Notes
Broad Dene* Hill Road	WF Unsworth	1900	Built for W Tyndale
Red Court* Scotlands Lane	Ernest Newton	1894-5	Built for Louis Wigram.
Red Court lodge* Scotlands Lane	Ernest Newton	c.1895	
Lythe Hill	FP Cockerell	1868	Built for Stuart Hodgson House demolished after fire
Courtyard Lodge,* **Hunters Lodge & Keepers** **Cottage** Haste Hill	FP Cockerell	c.1870 1887 late 20th c.	Only surviving part of Lythe Hill House Alterations
Oak Garth & The Garth* High Lane	JW Penfold	late 19th c.	Originally one house
Garth Cottage* High Lane	JW Penfold?	late 19th c.	Former stable for The Garth
Cleves* Weydown Road	EJ May?	early 20th c.	
Keffolds* Bunch Lane	H Hutchinson	1900/5	For Com Henderson. Now divided into three
Working Mens Club* Liphook Road, Shottermill	JW Penfold	1887	For Stuart Hudson Formally a school
Kemnal* Grayswood Road	Richard Norman Shaw RW Pite D Coombe	1888	Built for F Harrison Alterations
Kemnal Lodge* & **Kemnal Cottage***	Richard Norman Shaw Richard Norman Shaw	c.1883 c.1883	Twin lodges
Church of All Saints* **Grayswood**	Axel Haig, assisted by Oliver & Dodgson RF Macdonald	1901-2	Built for A Harman Internal alterations

Building	Architect	Date	Notes
Hindhead House* Off Hindhead Road, Hindhead	JW Penfold?	1884/5	For Prof Tyndall. Formally Tyndalls
Undershaw Hotel* Portsmouth Road, Hindhead	Joseph Henry Ball	1893	For Sir A Conan Doyle
Barn at High Pitfold* Farmhouse, Hindhead	Edwin Lutyens	early 20th c.	
Stable & Shelter Shed* at **High Pitfold Farm**,Hindhead	Edwin Lutyens	early 20th c.	
United Reformed Church,* **Hall & Manse** Hindhead	John Grover	1899	After sketch by RN Shaw
Church of St. Alban* Tilford Road, Hindhead	JD Coleridge	1907-10	
Jesses* Grayswood Road	Parbury	1918	Purchased for Arnold Dolmech Original Dolmech workshop
Amesbury School* Hazel Grove, Hindhead	Edwin Lutyens	1903	Built as The Mount for WG Jackson At some point called West Down
St. Edmunds School* **Formally Blencathra**	Dudley Newman Stedman & Blower	c.1895 post1945	G B Shaw lived here Refurbishment
Church of St. Stephen Shottermill	JW Penfold	1838 1876	Enlarged
Our lady of Lourdes RC Church	FA Walters	1924	
Honeyhanger	EJ May	c.1900	For CB McLaren, later Lord Aberconway
The Lodge	CFA Voysey	1904	
The Wellan Polecat Lane	CFA Voysey	1903	Formally pair of cottages called New Place Cottages. Southern cottage demolished, northern cottage rebuilt

Building	Architect	Date	Notes
Dickhurst	Charles Harrison Townsend	1894-5	Built for JH or EH Baker
Frensham Hall/St. Marys Abbey	C Ellis		
High Rough/Royal School	A Brownrigg		Built for AE Leon. RF Macdonald more likely architect
Pleylands	Herbert Read & Macdonald		
Great Stoatley	G Redmayne?		
Courts Hill	JW Penfold		Built for Miss Penfold
Scotlands	G Unsworth		
Methodist Church	HJ Orchard	1972	
Olivers Mill	JW Penfold		Repairs after fire
Cottage Hospital	JW Penfold	1898	Memorial to his parents
Penfold	JW Penfold	1898	Alterations for self
Womens Club	H Hutchinson		
Westminster Bank	A Brownrigg		
Blacksmiths Shop	JW Penfold		Conversion to house
The White House	WA Pite A Chandler	1880s	Alterations for Raynor Storr Conversion to Georgian Hotel
Tudor Cottage	WA Pite	1884	Alterations and restoration for Raynor Storr. Pite's first commission.
Museum Galleries	A Chandler		For Trustees of Haslemere Museum
Three Counties Club	A Chandler		Demolished 1994
Haslemere District Hospital Childrens ward Extensions Marjorie Gray Hall	Herbert Read & McDonald WA Pite, Son & Fairweather RW Pite RW Pite	1923	

Building	Architect	Date	Notes
Health Centre **Casualty Dept.**	J Watrach T Kline		Member of SW Thames Regional Health Board Architects Dept
St. Georges Wood	Robert Falconer Macdonald RW Pite		For his brother. Conversion to Maternity Unit Since converted to flats
School	Robert Falconer Macdonald	1904	
Grayshurst & Lodge	A Haig	1891	For self
Redcot	A Brownrigg		For B Day
The Small House	A Brownrigg		Built for self
The Fox & Pelican Grayshott	Robert Falconer Macdonald?	1899	
Chapel	Richard Norman Shaw?	1899	
The Croft	EJ May	1893	Built for Mr Grant Allen
Church of St. Joseph	FA Walters	1911	
Moorhouse	Edwin Lutyens D Coombe		Alterations
Pine House	Ernst Freud	1934	Concert room for Miss Gill Concert Room Cottage for W Wordsworth, composer
Stoatley Rough	Robert Falconer Macdonald	1896	
Vicarage	JD Coleridge	1910-11	
Highcombe Edge	WA Pite	1899	Built for Raynor Storr
Thirlestane	Richard Norman Shaw?		
The Cottage	HH Stannus?	1887	Built for self
Garages, Aldershot & District Traction co.	AJ Stedman		

Building	Architect	Date	Notes
Peperharow			
Church of St. Nicholas	AWN Pugin	1844	Probably Norman but mostly Pugin
Thursley Parish			
The Corner* Thursley Road	Edwin Lutyens	1888-9	Earlier Cottages converted into single house. For E Gray
Prospect Cottage* The Street	Edwin Lutyens	1900	Built as Village Institute for Rev. Gooch
Warrenmere* Portsmouth Road	Edwin Lutyens	1896-7	Was Warren Lodge. Rebuilt for Robert Webb.
Guest and Service Wing*	Edwin Lutyens	1909	Extended by Lutyens for Lord Stamfordham
Boathouse on Thursley Lake* Witley Park	Edwin Lutyens	1897	For Whitaker Wright
Church of St. Michael	Ferrey	1860	
	JW Penfold	1883-6	Rebuilt more or less
Cottages	Edwin Lutyens	1901	For Robert Webb
Tilford Parish			
Crooksbury House*} **Fig Tree Court}** **West Wing}** Crooksbury Road	Edwin Lutyens	1890-2 1898-9 1914	For WA Chapman New east wing New east wing & service wings for FE Briggs. Jekyll garden
Clock House & Crooksbury **House Cottage*** Crooksbury Road	Edwin Lutyens Edwin Lutyens	1890 1901	Formally Stable Court Rebuilt
Crooksbury House Lodge* Crooksbury Road	Edwin Lutyens	1890	
Church of All Saints* Tilford Road	Ewan Christian	1867	13th c. style

Building	Architect	Date	Notes
Tilford Institute* Tilford Road	Edwin Lutyens Michael Edwards	1893 1998-9	For Mrs Anderson Extended
Sheephatch House	Edwin Lutyens	1890	Built as Heathy Field. Additions for Mrs. Anderson
Tancredsford	Harold Falkner Stedman & Blower	c.1920	Alterations?
Greyfriars	E Turner Powell	c.1910	
C of E aided School, Key Cross	AJ & LR Stedman	post 1945	New Senior School

Witley Parish

Building	Architect	Date	Notes
Kingwood Hall,* **Kingwood Court*** **Kingwood Coach House*** Brook Road, Sandhills	FW Troup	1902	House now divided. Built for J King as Sandhouse
Kingwood Lodge* Brook Road, Sandhills	FW Troup	1902	For J King
Stable at Kingwood* Brook Road, Sandhills	FW Troup	1902	Now dwelling
9,11 & 15 Afton Cottages* Church Road, Milford	Edwin Lutyens	1898	Restored by Lutyens?
Brook Lodge* Witley Park Haslemere Road	Paxton Hood Watson	1896	For Whitaker Wright
Bonneville Spring* Milford Road, Elstead	AWN Pugin	1843	Folly building containing spring, now mostly destroyed. Built for 5th Viscount Midleton
Oxenford Gate Lodge* Milford Road	AWN Pugin	1843-4	
Barn at Oxenford Grange*	AWN Pugin	1843	

Building	Architect	Date	Notes
Granary and Farm Buildings* Oxenford Grange	AWN Pugin	1843	
King Edwards School* Petworth Road, Wormley	Sidney Smirke GD Sykes	1867	Extensions
Culmer Farm House* Petworth Road, Wormley	WD Caröe	20th c.	16th c. house remodelled in early 20th c. Later 20th c. additions at rear
Wood End* Petworth Road, Wormley	Edwin Lutyens	1897	Jekyll garden
Pinewood Brook Road, Wormley	Ralph Nevill	1870	Additions
Rake Manor & Rake Court* Station Lane, Milford	Ralph Nevill Edwin Lutyens Baillie Scott	1882 1897 1910/1925	Extension to 17th century House. Extensions Extensions
West Surrey Golf Club Enton, Milford	Arthur Albert Messer	1910	
Milford Lodge* Witley Park	Paxton Hood Watson	1896	Built for Whitaker Wright
Thursley Lodge* Witley Park	Paxton Hood Watson	1896	Built for Whitaker Wright
Stable Block* Witley Park	Paxton Hood Watson	1896	For Lea House
Bathing Pavilion* On Stable Lake, Witley Park	Edwin Lutyens	1897	
The Refectory Milford	Mr Flenning	1937	Former barn converted by Flenning
Barnacle Edge Sandhills, Witley	Basil Champneys	1893	
Witley Court	Birkett Foster	1861	Built as The Hill for Birkett Foster to his design

Building	Architect	Date	Notes
The Village Hall Milford	Baillie Scott	1922	

Wonersh Parish

Building	Architect	Date	Notes
Great Tangley Manor* & **Great Tangley Manor West***	Philip Webb George Jack Inigo Thomas	1886 1902 1906	Additions to earlier house Additions Addition of north wing, demolished 1948
Edgton Little Tangley	Edwin Lutyens	1890-92	Alterations to Little Tangley'sstables to form Edgton, for Cowley Lambert
Little Tangley	 Edwin Lutyens	1877 1899	 Additions
Chinthurst Hill,* **Close House and Gate House***	Edwin Lutyens	1893-5	For Miss Aemilia Guthrie
St. Johns Seminary*	FA Walters	1895	
Church of St. Martins* Blackheath	Charles Harrison Townsend	1895	For Sir William Robert-Austin
Greyfriars Franciscan Friary* Blackheath	FA Walters	1895	
Village Hall Blackheath	Charles Harrison Townsend	1897	
Chapel End Blackheath	Charles Harrison Townsend	1901	Former Congregational Chapel
Combe Green Blackheath	Charles Harrison Townsend	c.1902/7	Formally Blatchcombe
Theobalds Blackheath	Charles Harrison Townsend	c.1902/7	
The Vicarage Blackheath	Charles Harrison Townsend	c.1902/7	

Building	Architect	Date	Notes
Cobbins Blackheath	Charles Harrison Townsend	c.1902/7	
Cheshunt Blackheath	Charles Harrison Townsend	c.1902/7	
Cemetery Chapel Blackheath	Charles Harrison Townsend	c.1902/7	
Rosemary Hill Blackheath	Charles Harrison Townsend	c.1902/7	
Blatchfield Blackheath	Charles Harrison Townsend	c.1894	
Barnett Hill* Blackheath Lane	Arnold Mitchell	1904	Built for F Cook, now Red Cross Centre
Stable Block*	Arnold Mitchell	c.1905	
Lodge*	Arnold Mitchell	c.1905	
Christchurch* Shamley Green	C H Howell	1863/4	Later County Architect
Upper House*	Richard Norman Shaw	1874	Additions to earlier house
Stoke Allbrooke*,Waverley*	Richard Norman Shaw	1880	
Cottage & Magnolia Cottage* Shamley Green	Richard Norman Shaw	1887-8 20th c.	Further additions
The Hallams* Littleford Lane	Richard Norman Shaw	1894-5	For Charles Durant Hodgson
Arbuthnot Hall Shamley Green	Charles Harrison Townsend	1906	
Willinghurst*	Phillip Webb	1887	Built as Lapscombe for Capt Ramsden. Partly demolished in1950s
Coach House*, Little Willinghurst	Phillip Webb	1887	
Stroud Lodge* Willinghurst	Phillip Webb?	1899	20th c. Additions

Building	Architect	Date	Notes
Smithwood Common Lodge* Willinghurst	Phillip Webb?	1897	
Willinghurst Cottage*	Phillip Webb	1887-9	Earlier cottage extended
Derrys Wood	JF Bentley	1903-5	Built for Courage family
United Reform Church Wonersh Common	Howard Seth Smith	1880	
Church of St. John the Baptist	Henry Woodyer Sir Charles Nicholson	1901	Restoration Remodelling of east end and internal fittings
Wonersh Surgery The Street	Judith Ledeboer?		
Wonersh Pavilion The Common	Michael Hemmings	2000	
The Manor House Shamley Green	TG Jackson	1893-5	
Garden Close Shamley Green	Michael McLelland	1980s	For Waverley Borough Council
Winterden Shamley Green	Michael McLelland	1992	For Sir D & Lady Morpeth
Sceamel Mere Woodhill Lane, Shamley Green	Sir Geoffrey Jellicoe		

Bibliography
& textual acknowledgements

The Buildings of England – Surrey by Ian Nairn & Nikolaus Pevsner.
Penguin Books, 1999.

Arts & Crafts Architecture by Peter Davey.
Phaidon Press, 1995.
Quote on page 68 reproduced from Arts & Crafts Architecture © 1995 Phaidon Press Ltd.

Lutyens by The Arts Council of Great Britain.
1981.

Victorian Architecture by Roger Dixon & Stefan Muthesius.
Thames & Hudson, 1978.
Quote on page 28 reproduced from Victorian Architecture ©1978 Thames & Hudson.

Nature & Tradition – Arts & Crafts Architecture and Gardens in and around Guildford edited by John Davey.
Guildford Borough Council, 1993.

The Surrey Style by Roderick Gradidge.
Surrey Historic Buildings Trust, 1991.

Architects of the Arts & Crafts Movement by Margaret Richardson.
RIBA Drawings Series, Trefoil Books, 1983.

The English House through Seven Centuries by Olive Cook.
Whittet Books Ltd, 1983.
Quote on page 1 reproduced courtesy of Whittet Books Ltd.

The English House 1860-1914 by Gavin Stamp.
Building Centre, 1980.

Architecture after Modernism by Diane Ghirardo.
Thames & Hudson, 1996.

20th Century Architecture by Martin Pawley.
Architectural Press, 2000.

A Celebration of Architecture by Henry Chetwynd-Stapylton.
Surrey County Council, 1991.

Harold Falkner by Caroline Smith.
Farnham Museum.

Victorian Farnham by W Ewbank-Smith.
Phillimore, 1971.

Farnham in War and Peace by W Ewbank-Smith.
Phillimore, 1983.

Farnham – Buildings and People by Nigel Temple.
The Farnham Press, 1962.

Licensed Farnham by Jean Parratt.
Pollyphonics, 1994.

Farnham Past by Jean Parratt.
Phillimore, 1999.

Harold Falkner – Architect 1875-1963 by Margaret Brandon Jones
Unpublished, 1971.

Personal Reminiscences of Farnham Architect Harold Falkner by
Jenny Mukerji. The Arts & Crafts Movement in Surrey, 1999.

Rake Manor by Alan Bott.
Surrey Archaeological Collections vol 80.
1990.

Godalming Parish Church by Alan Bott.
1978.

Old Cottage and Domestic Architecture of South West Surrey by Ralph
Nevill. 1889.

The Work of Ernest Newton RA by William Godfrey Newton.
The Architectural Press, London, 1925.

The English House by Hermann Muthesius.
First English translation by Janet Seligman.
Crosby Lockwood Staples, London, 1979.

Albury Old Church by Philip Mainwaring Johnston.
Surrey Archaeological Collections vol 34, 1922.

Notes on The Local History of Peper Harow by Hon George C Broderick.
Surrey Archaeological Collections vol 7.
Quote on Page 12 reproduced courtesy of Surrey Archaeological Society

Recollections of Pugin by Benjamin Ferrey
Scholar Press, London, 1861.

Richard Scott, pers. comm.
2001.

Monumental Headache – Guildhall Yard. On site by James McNeil.
Building, September 1995.

Full Circle by Sutherland Lyall.
Building, December 1995.

Arts & Crafts Extremist – Charles Harrison Townsend by Alastair
Service.
Architectural Association Quarterly. Vol 6, 1974.

F W Troup Architect 1859-1941 by Neil Jackson.
Building Centre Trust, 1985.

Arts and Crafts Comes to Town by Neil Jackson.
Architects Journal, 1985.

Parsimonious Philanthropy - The Minor Architecture of F W Troup by
Neil Jackson.
RIBA Journal, 1985.

The Arts & Crafts Movement in Surrey; Westbrook by Lesley Price, 1997.

Hugh Thackeray Turner by Merilyn Spier. 1997.

Architectural Review LXX, 1931.

CFA Voysey by Stuart Durant, Architectural Monograph 19.
Academy Editions, London 1992.

C R Ashbee – Memoirs Vol VII.

The Work of the late Philip Webb by E L Lutyens.
Country Life XXXVII 1915.
Quote on page 42 reproduced courtesy of Country Life.

A History of Hascombe by Winifred D Ashton.
1999

Church of St Peter, Hascombe by Rev. Vernon Musgrave.
1885.

A Brief Account of the Life and Work of Henry Woodyer, 1816-1896
by Anthony Quiney. Architectural History, vol 38, 1995

Brave New World by Aldous Huxley
Chatto & Windus, 1994.
*Quote on page 70 from Brave New World by Aldous Huxley, published by
Chatto & Windus. Reprinted by permission of The Random House Group
Ltd.*

Demian by Hermann Hesse.
English Translation. Peter Owen Publishers 2001
Quoted courtesy of Peter Owen Ltd. London 2001.

William Morris - His Life & Work by Stephen Coote
Sutton Publishing Ltd. 1996
Quotes on pages 2,3 &4 courtesy of Sutton Publishing Ltd.

Index

Index

Index

Index

Index